HOW TO PROFITABLY
BUY AND SELL LAND

Real Estate for Professional Practitioners
A Wiley Series

DAVID CLURMAN, Editor

CONDOMINIUMS AND COOPERATIVES   by David Clurman and
Eda L. Hebard

THE BUSINESS CONDOMINIUM   by David Clurman

HOW TO PROFITABLY BUY AND SELL LAND   by Rene A. Henry, Jr.

HOW TO PROFITABLY BUY AND SELL LAND

RENE A. HENRY, JR.

Executive Officer
ICPR
Los Angeles, California

A WILEY-INTERSCIENCE PUBLICATION

JOHN WILEY & SONS
NEW YORK • LONDON • SYDNEY • TORONTO

This publication is designed to provide accurate and
authoritative information in regard to the subject
matter covered. It is sold with the understanding that
the publisher is not engaged in rendering legal, accounting, or other professional service. If legal advice or
other expert assistance is required, the services of a
competent professional person should be sought.
*From a Declaration of Principles jointly adopted by a
Committee of the American Bar Association and a Committee
of Publishers.*

Library of Congress Cataloging in Publication Data:
Henry, Rene A., Jr.
  How to profitably buy and sell land.

  (Real estate for professional practitioners)
  "A Wiley-Interscience publication."
  1. Real estate-investment—United States.   2. Real
estate investment.   I. Title.

HD1375.H46   332.6'324'0973   76-22522
ISBN 0-471-37291-9

Printed in the United States of America

10 9 8 7 6 5 4 3 2 1

To

MOTHER and **BILL**
DEBBIE and **BRUCE**

SERIES PREFACE

Since the end of World War II, tremendous changes have taken place in the business and residential real estate fields throughout the world. This has been evidenced not only by architectural changes, exemplified by the modern shopping center, but also in the many innovative financing responses that have enabled development of new structures and complexes, such as multiuse buildings. It can be expected that new directions in real estate development will speed at an ever increasing pace to match the oncoming needs of our time. With this perspective, The Real Estate for Professional Practitioners has been developed in response to professional needs.

As real estate professional activities have become divided into specialties, because of intensive demand for expertise at all stages, so has there developed an increasing need for extensive training and continual education for persons directly involved or dealing in business ventures requiring detailed knowledge of realty procedures.

Perhaps no field of business endeavor is more in need of a series of professional books than real estate. Working in the practical world of business and residential construction and space utilization, or at advanced levels of college training covering these areas, one is constantly aware that too little of existing creative thinking has been transcribed into viable books. Many of the books that have been written do not thoroughly enough encompass both the practical and theoretical aspects of complex subjects. Too often the drive for immediate answers has led to the overlooking of fundamental purposes and technical know-how that might lead to much more favorable results for the persons seeking knowledge.

This series will be made up of books thoroughly and expertly expounding existing procedures in the many fields of real estate, but searching as well for innovative solutions to current and future problems. These books are intended to offer a compendium of each author's wide experience and knowledge to aid the seasoned professional.

The series is addressed to professionals in all walks of realty endeavor. These include business investors and developers, urban affair specialists, attorneys, and the many others whose work involves real estate creativity and investment. Just as importantly, the series will present to advanced students in many realty fields the opportunity to review professional thinking that will help to stimulate their own thoughts on modern trends in housing and business construction.

We believe these goals can be achieved by the outstanding group of authors who will create the books in the series.

DAVID CLURMAN

ACKNOWLEDGMENTS

The author wishes to thank and acknowledge the following industry leaders and organizations whose efforts helped make this book possible:

Irwin M. Adler, President, Carol Housing Corp., Miami, Fla.
Kenneth W. Agid, Director of Residential Marketing, The Irvine Co., Newport Beach, Calif.
Kurt Alexander, Partner, Kenneth Leventhal & Co., Los Angeles, Calif.
William Baker, President, Florida Land Co., a wholly owned subsidiary of Florida Gas Company, Winter Park, Fla.
William Becker, William E. Becker & Associates, Inc., Paramus, N.J.
Martin S. Berger, President, Robert Martin Corp., Elmsford, N.Y.
Barry A. Berkus, AIA, Santa Barbara, Calif.
Steve Berlinger, Kenneth Leventhal & Co., Los Angeles, Calif.
Eli Broad, Chairman, Kaufman and Broad, Inc., Los Angeles, Calif.
Ford R. Carter, Ford R. Carter, Inc., Delray Beach, Fla.
David Clurman, Phillips, Nizer, Benjamin, Krim & Ballon, New York, N.Y.
Council of Housing Producers, Los Angeles, Calif.
William O. Doherty, American Institute of Certified Public Accountants, New York, N.Y.
Patty Doyle, Patty Doyle Public Relations, Ft. Lauderdale, Fla.
Robert Martin Englebrecht, AIA, architect, Princeton, N.J.
Louis E. Fischer, President, General Development Corp., Miami, Fla.
Ronald R. Foell, President, Standard-Pacific Corp., Costa Mesa, Calif.
John Galvin, Senior Vice President, Aetna Life & Casualty Company, Hartford, Conn.
Sanford R. Goodkin, Sanford R. Goodkin Research Corp., Del Mar, Calif.
Maurice A. Hall, Beverly Hills, Calif. and Bahia Chamela, Jalisco, Mexico
John Holmes, Ford R. Carter, Inc., Delray Beach, Fla.
Pancho Hunt, Partner, Lincoln Property Co., Santa Monica, Calif. and Compañia Mexicana de Fomento Urbanistico, Guadalajara, Jalisco, Mexico
Michael I. Keston, President, The Larwin Group, Inc., Encino, Calif.
Hon. John V. N. Klein, County Executive, Suffolk County, Hauppauge, N.Y.
Harry Kwartler, Partner, Archer Development Co., Paramus, N.J.
Michael McCloskey, Executive Director, The Sierra Club, San Francisco, Calif.
Jackson McDaniel, McDaniel Development Corp., Orlando, Fla.
Nathan J. Miller, Chairman, Building and Land Technology Corp., Ft. Lee, N.J.
Dallas Miner, The Urban Land Institute, Washington, D.C.
National Association of Home Builders, Washington, D.C.
William Nolan, Residential Consultants, Philadelphia, Penna.

Bruce Nott, Newport Beach, Calif.

Bonnie O'Brien, Society of Real Estate Appraisers, Chicago, Ill.

Richard W. O'Neill, President, Housing Advisory Council, Ltd., Lakeville, Conn.

William R. Phillips, A.S.L.A., Phillips, Brandt, Reddick and Associates, Inc., Irvine, Calif.

LeNore Plotkin, Title Insurance & Trust Co., Los Angeles, Calif.

Paul Pohly, Paul T. Pohly & Company, Dallas, Texas

David Price, Executive Vice President, National Homes Corp., Lafayette, Indiana

Samuel Primack, Partner, The Perl-Mack Companies, Denver, Colo.

David Riese, President, Development Group of America, Ft. Lauderdale, Fla.

Stan Ross, Partner, Kenneth Leventhal & Co., Los Angeles, Calif.

Carl A. Rudnick, President, R&M Financial Corp., Los Angeles, Calif. a joint enterprise with The Richards Group, Inc., an affiliate of Gulf & Western Industries, Inc.

Charles Rutenberg, Chairman, U.S. Home Corp., Clearwater, Fla.

Ralph Shirley, Ralph Shirley Investments, Houston, Texas

Gail Stoorza, The Gail Stoorza Company, La Jolla, Calif.

Gary A. Terry, Executive Vice President, American Land Development Association, Washington, D.C.

U.S. Department of Housing & Urban Development, Washington, D.C.

Robert Volk, President, Unionamerica Corp., Los Angeles, Calif.

Richard Wasserman, Partner, The Richards Group, a joint venture with Gulf & Western, Great Neck, N.Y.

Richard Weiss, Partner, The Richlar Partnership, Beverly Hills, Calif.

F. Thomas Winters, III, Partner, Agvest/Verdex, Beverly Hills, Calif.

Lewis N. Wolff, Partner, Wolff-Sesnon Development Co., Los Angeles, Calif.

The author especially appreciates and wishes to acknowledge the efforts involved in research coordination by Margaret E. Eriksen.

PREFACE

At some time all of us have probably heard or read stories of how investors have gotten rich quick by investing in land. However, we seldom learn of the risks involved in land investment or of the losses an owner incurs who purchases a piece of land that should never have been acquired.

We have all heard: "Land has a greater profit potential than any other kind of investment." "One good land investment can equal a lifetime of work." "Land is the only true hedge against inflation." Each of these statements is valid, taken in the proper context and considering the time when it is made.

Although cities, towns, and villages occupy less than two percent of the nation's total land mass, land is and has always been an expensive and a critical factor in new development. Following World War II and until the economic recession of the mid-1970s, no other element in the development and construction process increased faster than the percentage increase in the land cost component of the final cost of a house or building.

Today land investment and acquisition is a complex business. An investor can no longer buy land and simply sit back and do nothing but wait for its immediate appreciation. Elected and appointed government officials and policy makers currently exercise strong regulatory powers over when and how land can be used. The emotional attitudes and concerted efforts of environmentalists and ecologists have had a further telling impact on when, how, and even *if* land can be developed.

Moreover, land planners, architects, and designers have introduced more creative and professional land-use concepts in recent years. New earthmoving equipment that virtually can move mountains; the ability to reclaim swamp and marshlands once believed to be unbuildable; the redevelopment of the nation's urban areas; and advances in transportation systems and technology all make land acquisition today a complex and sophisticated investment.

Essential to successful land investment are: the timing of the acquisition; the selectivity in the location of the property; the availability of financial resources; the compilation of market research to support the profitability and political feasibility of the development; and professional planning.

Within view of the Pacific Ocean, for example, there is enough room to house the entire U.S. population, with a density of less than 15 people to an acre! However, much of this now-vacant land may never be developed because of the no-growth attitudes of regulatory agencies or is not developable because it is inaccessible to public transportation.

A 1975 study by C. George Ross, a University of California researcher, reported that California alone contained 448,000 vacant lots and parcels of recreation land that comprised a total area larger than the state of Rhode Island. At the current rate of development this is a sufficient supply to sustain recreational and vacation house sites for the next 50 years or more in California.

The marketability of land is directly related to the demand for a particular parcel of land. Many contemporary economists and financial advisors would have argued with Winston Churchill in 1922 when he said: "... [land] is the original source of all wealth ...", and "Land monopoly is not the only monopoly, but it is by far the greatest of monopolies—it is a perpetual monopoly, and it is the mother of all forms of monopoly." It is questionable whether Churchill would have made these statements in the perspective of current land economics.

The term "environmental impact report" was unheard of in 1922 and was not to be defined for more than half a century. The balance sheets and the financial losses of many large real estate development companies burdened with the costs of massive inventories of raw land quickly dispel the "monopoly" theory today.

Unlike any other investment, the purchase of raw land in itself is a unique venture. The word "deal" has become synonymous with land acquisition, because no set guidelines or published prices exist for the purchase of real estate as for stocks and bonds or consumer products.

A land investment is a "deal" in the sense that the principals virtually make up their own rules. The selling price of a piece of raw land is what a buyer is willing to pay for it. The terms and conditions are those agreed on by the buyer and the seller.

As is true of most real estate transactions, a land transaction requires the ultimate financial creativity of industry professionals, who must determine how a purchase can be structured to obtain maximum benefit for the buyer and the seller. It is extremely important for all parties involved in a land transaction to secure the best possible professional advice and counsel.

A buyer of raw land should follow certain procedures and safeguards in any acquisition. This book contains some general guidelines and checklists to be followed in purchasing land. Ideas and concepts that have proved successful are documented in case histories and examples of the acquisitions of some leading industry professionals.

One word of caution, however. A potential investor must remember that a land transaction is unlike any other business transaction. Because some concept worked well for someone at some particular time and place, does not necessarily mean that it will automatically work for another person at another time under different or even similar circumstances. No formula for a land transaction can be learned in a business school or documented in any book as the *only* way to conduct or close real estate negotiations. For this reason it is most important that the sophisticated investor rely on the advice of experienced legal and financial professionals.

This book reflects the viewpoints and ideas of highly successful professionals and entrepreneurs in the real estate industry. It is primarily written for people who are directly involved in the industry, but the book should also apply and appeal to high-income earners and sophisticated investors who are interested in land investment. Moreover, the book provides a useful checklist and reference for anyone who is involved in a land transaction.

In connection with the writing of this book, including the excerpts quoted from experts in the field, I have made every effort to be as accurate as possible and to secure their approval for use of such statements, and I alone am responsible for the accuracy thereof.

RENE A. HENRY, JR.

Los Angeles
May 1976

CONTENTS

CHAPTER XIV

GOVERNMENT REGULATION   137

CHAPTER XV

FOREIGN INVESTMENT OPPORTUNITIES   152

CHAPTER I

FINDING LAND

Finding land to buy is never a problem. Land is always for sale regardless of economic conditions. Newspapers contain columns of daily advertisements describing land investment opportunities. Almost every day we see an on-site sign somewhere offering a piece of land for sale.

Finding the *right* land to buy, however, is just as difficult in a recession as in a bullish economy. Simply stated, finding the *right* land means finding land without encumbrances, at the right price, that can be purchased at favorable terms, that has appreciation potential, that does not have any foreseeable usability risks, and that meets the investment or development objectives of the buyer.

Generally, professionals in the real estate industry never buy land unless they have a specific need or use for the property, thus virtually eliminating the risk of short-term speculation. Before purchasing real estate usually the land broker, agent, or deal-maker identifies a buyer to whom the land can be resold. The developer or builder previously identifies his need or specific use for a piece of land and verifies that it meets his plans and objectives.

Acquiring land without any specific need is categorized as *speculation.* Such a purchaser would best be defined as a speculator. If the land sufficiently appreciates in value to realize a favorable capital gain and return based on the amount and time of the investment, then the "speculator" realistically can call himself an "investor."

1

SOURCES OF AVAILABLE LAND

Opportunities to find land are numerous. The manner in which land is found usually varies according to objective and need. A large real estate developer or building company may make a specific staff member responsibile for finding land. A medium-sized or smaller company may work through a consultant or a broker who serves the same management function. An individual who wishes to invest or speculate in land may either do so himself or work through a broker-agent friend. Similarly, a consultant or broker-agent who works on behalf of a client, follows a procedure identical to the individual investor seeking land to buy.

Individuals or Families. Perhaps the single most important source of available land to date and in the next decade will be individuals. Large acreage for residential use is suburban or rural land that once was agricultural. Much of this land has been farmed by a family for several generations. Urban land suited for commercial or industrial development is also likely to be owned by an individual, but this trend is changing now and will continue to change in the years ahead.

Companies. Whether they are corporations, partnerships, or joint ventures, publicly or privately held, real estate oriented or not, companies are also a prime source of saleable land. During the residential housing boom in the early 1970s, many builders acquired great amounts of land so quickly that they became "land poor" and did not realize their mistake until the housing market plummeted into a down cycle in 1973. Conglomerates that acquired real estate companies and subsequently either terminated or drastically reduced the level of their development activity have found themselves inheriting sizable land inventories. Other large companies such as public utilities, those involved in the exploration as well as retailing of petroleum products, railroads that have held title to land for years, corporate farming operations, and even retailers of consumer products today have more land than can be projected or planned for specific use.

Government. Federal, state, and local governments are important but lesser known and utilized sources of land. Certain government agencies or public entities also have acquired more land than they need and in the case of escalating budgets may sell land parcels to increase income. A city may defer constructing a new park or a public building and may sell a downtown building site. School boards may sell unneeded land if ten-year projections for expansion are not realized. Urban development and redevelopment funds enable local city governments to acquire and market land based on a tax-increment formula that returns more tax dollars to the city where there is a greater potential for new development. Highway departments may decide to reroute freeways, and land they currently own may no longer be usable for their projections.

Lenders. Commercial banks, savings and loan associations, and other thrift institutions, real estate investment trusts, and life insurance companies, much to their dislike, become large land owners during recessions in the real estate industry. Some land parcels can be purchased during foreclosure sales. Depending on a particular lender's land inventory, a price may not be the bargain one would expect. Smart lenders inventory the land they acquire through loan defaults or foreclosures and try to recoup at least their profit margins, hopefully more, when the recessionary cycle turns around and a demand again exists for buildable land.

Realtors, Brokers, and Agents. Any licensed real estate agent is an intermediary who works for the buyer and is paid by the seller when the transaction is consummated. The seller may list land exclusively with an agent, and it is important for the buyer to determine to whom the agent is obligated. Most professionals in the real estate industry believe that a professional whose business it is to acquire land should also assist in buying the land. Given specific objectives, a knowledgeable, experienced, successful broker can provide a buyer with available land opportunities more quickly and more economically than the buyer could doing it himself.

Syndicates. Syndicates provide capital gains and some tax shelter by pooling the financial resources of several or many individual land holders. A syndicate can be either privately or publicly-held and can be a large group or a handful of people. The land held by a syndicate can be a specific parcel or a pooling of several parcels. Generally, land is held by a syndicate to obtain short-term capital gains of less than five years. The typical syndicate is structured to meet the investment objectives of the partner investors.

FINDING THE LAND

Ralph Shirley, Houston land broker, looks for land that is hopefully going to appreciate in value in the first two months, but in a maximum of three years. "I would never buy a piece of dirt if I didn't think it was going to appreciate 100% in six months," Shirley states. "I never have and never will buy land if I can't stand on it and see development getting ready to happen."

Shirley believes that to obtain maximum appreciation land should be purchased at the time development begins. The best land investment opportunities are in growth-oriented, metropolitan areas.

"When I seek out land to buy, I assume every piece of dirt or raw ground is for sale," Shirley says. "All I have to do is meet that guy's price." Here are some of the research tools and methods that Shirley uses to find land:

• A map book that contains drawings and surveys of various land parcels located in a city or a county and the names of the land owners. Private companies publish map books for various U.S. cities and counties; these books can be purchased by the general public.
• Public records, generally filed in the county courthouse, that list the abstract numbers of lots or parcels and the names and addresses of the owners of record.
• Information on zoning requirements, obtainable from the local government agency responsible for planning and zoning. Zoning requirements are constantly updated by the government agency; they indicate what can be built and approved building locations.
• City or county traffic-count reports on major thoroughfares, indicating which streets are gaining traffic and where.
• Real estate sections of local newspapers, government and industry association bulletins, newsletters and publications, business newspapers and magazines, and industry trade magazines publish trends and significant announcements by large builders or successful developers regarding future plans in specific areas.
• Census reports that contain vital information and project population growth areas.
• Constantly updated aerial photographs recording grading or clearing activities. In areas where burning is still allowed, such activity often can be detected by the sight of smoke.
• Statistical information regarding the area, obtainable from the local chamber of commerce. In larger metropolitan areas additional chambers of commerce often exist in specific communities within a city.
• Rental occupancy figures as an indicator of growth. The fact that apartments are 98% full in an area on the outskirts of a city may indicate potential new jobs and new construction.
• Personal contact observations from flying over and driving around

areas. Talk with title insurance company executives, engineers, architects, surveyors, lenders, builders, developers, and other real estate agents and brokers. Look for survey stakes and red flags, indicators of pending activity in an area.

• A composite map, probably the single most important and confidential tool, started from scratch and revised almost daily. The composite map identifies all the land in an area by code numbers and notes all existing and proposed subdivisions and other coded information of significance to the user. Each code number refers to information contained in a book that includes the name, address, and telephone number of the owner; the name, address, and telephone number of the owner's broker or agent, if there is a listing; the asking price for the land; the most recent time the land has been sold and the sales price; and how the land is zoned. Where there is adjacent improved property, other reference information related to the code number indicates the selling prices of surrounding residences and how they have risen in value; the selling prices of rental apartments and commercial and industrial property; and income data on a unit or square-foot basis and how often there has been a transaction. Brochures, pamphlets, and other types of information available on the land are kept in a reference file according to the code number and so noted in the book. Such a composite map enables its user to immediately tell a client or a potential land buyer the prices, availability, and trends of land in a particular area.

WORKING WITH A BROKER

Most professional builders, developers, and industry consultants prefer to work with brokers and agents. A good broker performs a specific function: he spends all of his time finding and buying land. He is a specialist who can do his job better than anyone else.

"Good brokers have saved my clients hundreds of thousands of dollars buying land," says Paul T. Pohly, a Dallas industry consultant. "The broker negotiates the deal for you and will most likely work it out the way you want. A one-on-one deal with a buyer-user who is entering a new market and the seller almost never works out."

A real estate or a building company that is established in a market for a number of years is more likely to buy land directly from the owners. When these companies employ brokers, they are known from past experience.

Sometimes even when a company can negotiate a land purchase itself in the market area it knows best, it may prefer to use a broker. This happens when a company wants to remain anonymous, either because it is packaging several pieces of land to make a larger parcel or because it is concerned that its name, net worth, or reputation could result in a higher asking price.

Carl A. Rudnick of R&M Financial, Los Angeles, advises that a client never alienate a broker. "You also can't afford to work with one exclusively all the time. Look at every deal, and listen to the brokers who come to you." In some cases we may check out the ground ourselves and even determine who the owner is, and then ask a broker to act as a middleman for the negotiations."

When buying land in a new market, it is extremely important to work through a broker. A good broker or agent can be determined by reputation. Talk with mortgage companies and real estate departments of banks. If the same name reappears on different lenders' lists, this can be considered an indication of a good reputation.

"When I go into a city I'm not totally familiar with, one of the first things I do is to retain the best real estate attorney available," says Bruce E. Nott of Newport Beach, California. "Find out from him what is happening in the city, who to use as your consultants, and let him direct you to one or two qualified brokers."

David Riese of the Development Group of America, Ft. Lauderdale, finds one technique especially successful when seeking ten-acre sites for projects of 150–300 apartments. When Riese finds a general vicinity that may meet his requirement, he looks for the natural boundaries. "These might include a canal or wash, a freeway, railroad tracks or, other such obstacle that would impede natural ingress and egress to the site," says Riese. "The boundaries also may dictate how the project can be situated on the land. This is important to adapt our formulas that have proved successful on other projects." Riese prefers rectangular sites where the depth of the parcel is twice the length of its frontage. First he drives through an area, looking for all the noticeable pitfalls in a particular location. Then Riese flies over the area in a helicopter, starting in the center of the piece of land he is considering and spiraling out in a concentric, circular sweep of the entire general area.

STYLE TO THE LEVEL OF THE SELLER

When discussing a listing or a purchase with a land owner, it is necessary to know and understand his needs as well as his style and level of sophistication. This is particularly important when negotiating purchases of rural land.

"When I see a farmer, I wear a windbreaker and sport shirt. I plan on sitting around in his kitchen and talking. I don't drive my big Cadillac. I drive my small, three-year-old Mustang convertible," says Harry Kwartler of Archer Development Co., Paramus, N.J.

"Building credibility and confidence is primary. Once the individual has accepted me, my proposition is more acceptable. One of the things I always will tell a seller is "If you don't feel comfortable with me, and don't believe in what I am going to do, don't do business with me."

"A broker or buyer has to understand that if someone has lived on a piece of land, there is an emotional attachment which totally transcends logic, and the buyer that approaches this prospective seller on a logical basis is a fool. He must calm his emotional problems first. Deal with it in the framework of your business needs," Kwartler recommends.

WHEN AND HOW MUCH TO BUY?

"When money is sensitive and market conditions and the economy are questionable, only buy land with direction and a specific use," Martin S. Berger of the Robert Martin Corporation, Elmsford, N.Y. advises. "Over the years, however, we have bought many parcels at very low prices per acre with no specific use and have considered a five-year hold on the land."

According to Berger, direction does not necessarily mean immediate development. Direction can also mean a five-year hold, but the specific purchase must meet the management objectives of the company.

"I don't encourage anyone who goes into a land investment with me to plan for less than a five-year carry, regardless of what the current market conditions are," says Jackson McDaniel of McDaniel Development Corporation, Orlando, Florida. "There are so many factors that affect our use of land other than the simple demand for housing that the primary consideration is planning for the bust or planning for the boom. The boom and bust has become a function of government policy and political machinations more than a function of demand."

Most real estate and building companies only purchase the amount of land they actually need, based on an analysis of the market and an identification of the type of project, its scheduled development, and the cost allocation for land acquisition.

"There are only a couple of instances where I've bought more land than I needed," adds Bruce Nott. "In these instances the seller gave me terms that made it attractive for me to buy more land than I needed and put me in a position to speculate with his land and his money for a long period of time. This is the only condition under which I would speculate for an ongoing building operation."

Nott also believes that down cycles in the industry provide tremendous opportunities for buying close-in real estate previously scheduled to be developed 12–18 months when current market and economic conditions may preclude any development.

"I may look to the builder who has to liquidate to his lender and get the best terms I could. I would put myself in a five-to-ten-year hold position with as little principal as I could possibly put down, with the majority of the carry cost being interest and taxes," states Nott. "Anytime money eases and development activity begins, the pressure and demand for good, buildable land starts another cycle. The time to sell is at sometime during the rise of this cycle."

"When considering a new market area, often it is wise to let someone else prove it out first before making any major commitment," according to Louis E. Fischer, General Development Corporation, Miami. "You should always consider some pioneering in new markets, but don't do it with thousand-acre parcels. Start with a small parcel that can be built out in 18 months. It's much easier then to back off and back away."

Ralph Shirley believes he can make more money with the right small tract than he can with a 200- or 300-acre parcel:

A ten-acre tract is easier to sell than a 100-acre tract. I like to find out where a major developer is planning to purchase a 200- to 400-acre tract for development and tie up a small tract next door or across the street. Or, even better, find eight or ten 20- to 50-acre tracts that can be packaged for sale subject to a favorable engineering report.

I try to find a major developer who will develop this property, and hold back one or two of the tracts, with the developers knowledge, of course, for my own personal investment.

Our acquisition formula is based on never paying above 50% of what a developer or user can pay for this type of property. Even then we want to acquire the land under the terms of a no-personal-liability arrangement with the landowner. Ideally, we pay one year's prepaid interest plus a small amount of principal (say, 3% down). Interest-only payments should continue for as long as possible, hopefully five years.

You never know how you can buy, until you try.

LOOK FOR MARKET OPPORTUNITIES

Even in the most depressed real estate markets land investment opportunities can be found. "You need to identify a market need—

something that is not being fulfilled in the marketplace—and be the first to do it," says Irwin Adler of the Carol Housing Corporation, Miami. "This can be from either a national or a local standpoint. You need to create a product that will make a sufficient marketing impact to capture either all or a disproportionate share of the market to be successful. Then you look for the land that will make that possible."

This philosophy can be adapted to the purchase of virtually any type of urban or suburban real estate. Adler cites a residential opportunity he identified during the over-built situation in Miami and Southern Florida in 1974 and 1975. Although the real estate and housing market was depressed at that time, Adler recognized the need for a product that would appeal to successful professional people in the $40,000–60,000 salary range who were in their mid-40s and early 50s and approaching the "empty-nester" status:

> They didn't want high-rise living, would be turned off by a retirement community, and no longer needed a single-family house. We identified the need, then found a ten-acre parcel in a prestige area ten minutes from downtown Miami, and created an 80-unit, luxury townhouse project.

BUYING FROM CORPORATE CONGLOMERATES

Professional consultants who are knowledgeable in local markets can evaluate the importance of top-management decisions. They are most valuable in solving the problems of multimillion dollar corporations that are not real estate oriented.

"When I see an ad of a corporation listing land for sale, I feel they are unloading property and I can make a deal," says Paul Pohly. "The price put in the paper or quoted on the telephone has no relationship to the price they will accept.

"Any large corporation can save money with a good consultant. They'll save money whatever they pay him. The consultant has to advise the top management because too often staff people get too imbued with corporate philosophy and opinions of superiors to be objective."

Pohly cites an example where his firm was retained for a consulting fee of $6000 to evaluate a land purchase. A corporation was advised to purchase 400 acres of land at $5000 per acre, based on Pohly's evaluation of the land's worth at $20,000 per acre, or a difference of $2 million cost on an appraised market value of $8 million. Within 60 days the company sold 200 acres (half its holdings) for $10,000 per acre and recouped the $2 million cost. In six months the same land resold to another party for $17,000 per acre, or $3.4 million; six months later the land resold again, this time for $25,000 per acre, or $5 million. Within 14 months the parcel representing a $1 million original cost sold for $5 million. Within two years the same 200 acres resold once again, this time for $33,000 per acre, or $6.6 million, but even this figure was economically feasible for the projected development.

Ralph Shirley comments:

One of the greatest profit opportunities for a land man, is to search out property owned by major corporations. It is almost impossible for a major corporation to constantly be aware of the value of its raw land holdings. They cannot hire and keep the qualified people to stay on top of their properties. The staff people just do not do the research and field work necessary to constantly update happenings in the raw-land marketplace; in addition, they do not search out the inside information necessary to properly evaluate when to buy or when to sell.

People making the buy or sell decisions are not going to the right people to get their advice. They may order up-to-date land appraisals, but they do not understand the inner problems of the land business.

Our research department only accepts consulting and research assignments in the north and northwest sections of Harris County. Even though we office in Houston, we can only be totally knowledgeable in this general area. Other firms have our equal qualifications in south and southeast Houston.

In one case we purchased land for a client at $6500 an acre, when three adjacent landowners the week before had turned down between $20,000 and $25,000 an acre for similar land. The board of directors for the corporation decided they had too much land and they would immediately divest a certain percentage of land holdings. The staff man was told to "Take what you can get for it." We couldn't believe it when our offer was accepted at that price!

Decisions regarding what land to buy or sell and what price to pay or ask should be made only at the highest management levels of a large organization, according to Richard L. Weiss of the Richlar Partnership, Beverly Hills. "The staff man is your bird dog. He takes the guidelines you give him and will work with a local broker who will give advice on pros and cons and value. When the transaction is made, however, the responsibility and decision must be by a principal or very senior executive."

CHAPTER II

RESEARCH AND ANALYSIS

Finding land that can be purchased is only one of the many processes involved in land acquisition. Once found, land must be carefully evaluated through research and analysis to determine whether it meets the specific use or investment objectives of the buyer. Is the land the *right* land? What are the downside investment risks? What are the profit opportunities?

To protect against the possible loss of land to another buyer, when a buyer or an agent finds a lot or parcel that appears to meet all the buyer's requirements, he generally enters into a purchase contract, subject to various contingencies. Such a contract grants the buyer a specific period of time to further evaluate the land to determine if it is exactly what he wants before a final commitment to buy is made. This particular aspect of land acquisition and contract contingencies is covered in more detail in Chapter V.

Whether an outside consultant or the actual buyer conducts research and analysis, various elements must be weighed in consideration of the investment and development objectives. Many questions must be raised and answered.

An individual or an investment group making a land-speculation purchase is interested in whether the land will appreciate, how much it will appreciate, and over what period of time it will appreciate. The investor will also want to consider types of potential buyers for the property. A real estate company may be interested in the profit

11

potential of developing the land, reselling it using other marketing methods, or otherwise improving the value of the property.

Most large real estate building and development companies can conduct their own market research by following the same steps as those of a consultant. However, the staff person, who probably is totally company oriented, may have preconceived ideas or may be pressured by a superior to support management's views. An outside consultant is an objective, independent third party. Lenders also place significant importance on the consultant's recommendations and may ask their own research consultant to substantiate the report submitted by a builder or developer.

Some companies conduct their own quantitative analysis, which is primarily comprised of statistical data gathering and organization, and then retain a consultant to verify their data and to provide qualitative input. Qualitative analysis may be the most important contribution a consultant can make, which is why careful consideration should be given to the consultant to be retained.

A number of nationally recognized independent consulting firms provide land research and analysis for many leading companies, including those involved in building and development as well as lenders and public utilities. Included in this group are William E. Becker & Associates, Inc., Paramus, N.J.; Sanford R. Goodkin Research Corporation, Del Mar, California; Richard W. O'Neill's Housing Advisory Council, Ltd., Lakeville, Connecticut; Paul T. Pohly & Company, Dallas; Smolkin, Bost, and Miestchovich, New Orleans; and Robert L. Siegel & Associates, New Orleans.

Before hiring a consulting firm, its references should be checked. The firm can be asked for client references; clients can then be interviewed about specific projects. The lender who loaned money for the project and even the ultimate buyer or investment group, especially in the case of income-producing property, can also be contacted to determine how well the consultant did his job. If the projections are correct, the consultant can be retained based on his past performance.

Martin S. Berger clearly states the case concerning the use of consultants. "If I buy a parcel of land five miles from my office in Westchester, I try to take the view that I'm from California. I've got to learn everything possible about this parcel. I don't go by my own experience and emotional attitudes. I spend money in advance of the purchase to get good planning and research studies. Then I use my experience to cull these studies and to make sure the information is valid."

Consultant Paul Pohly asks a client very pointed questions about his financial capabilities, his ability to develop the project, how he envisions his plans, and his staying power. "The project should be conceived only in principle before the land is acquired. No building company should spend money on plans or architectural drawings and then try to find the land to fit the project. The consultant's research and recommendations should advise and give direction to the architect."

Harry Kwartler suggests really getting to know the seller. "Regardless of the type of property, find out if the seller has children, where they are living, and what their needs are. If you're looking at farm property in Pennsylvania and the farmer has a son living in Detroit and a daughter in Washington, it's pretty logical that they're not going to want to come back and run the farm. But if he has two sons, both living on the farm, you had better address yourself to those sons and tell them they are going to have a lot to say."

DATA GATHERING

To obtain the necessary information to thoroughly research and analyze a land acquisition requires returning to many of the same sources that were consulted in finding the land. A researcher, whether on the company staff or an independent consultant, takes a different viewpoint in evaluating property than a broker or an agent does in finding available land.

Paul Pohly believes a good market researcher should become even more familiar with a town or a community than a local builder, developer, or broker. "He is flexible in his approach and will go in assuming he is going to be brainwashed. The analyst's position is to go in, listen and gather statistics, and then evaluate them. There are statistics that are important, but you've got to weed through the propaganda," Pohly advises.

Before entering a town or community, the researcher must know names of several important people. One of these people—usually a senior officer in charge of the real estate department of a bank—is the starting point. Some consultants believe it is better just to walk in rather than make an appointment for the interview, because people generally are more accommodating to a visitor from out of town with limited time. The first contact should recommend other contacts, including developers, mortgage bankers, and other bankers. The analyst should try to obtain candid answers about the community's economy and the composition of the town.

Lenders are an excellent source of comparable data, particularly if the land being acquired is to be developed as income-producing real estate. Lenders can not only provide information on the availability and cost of mortgages, but also on comparable projects, square footage, cost, amenities, cost of maintenance and utilities, and taxes.

The local government is another important source of information pertaining to land acquisition. The analyst may talk with the mayor, city councillors, the city manager, and officials in the planning and building departments. In most cities recent studies, maps, photographs, and plans can be purchased. The analyst must also determine if the local government is stable: Who is up for reelection and when? Is there a history of zoning rollbacks? Is there currently any pressure on local politicians or official departments to enact moratoriums or zoning rollbacks that could negate the potential value of the land? Is this a political environment in which objectives can be achieved in the projected or established timetable? What is the risk or vulnerability of the local political climate? What use permits or variances may be required? What is the working relationship between the local government and regional or federal regulatory agencies that require environmental impact reports and Environmental Protection Agency Clean Air Standards. The analyst must obtain a transportation and traffic study and study these plans to determine if any changes or additions are to be made in major arterial freeways, thoroughfares, or streets that could affect or impede ingress and egress from the property.

The analyst must also evaluate the growth patterns of an area. For planned residential use of the land, the growth area is generally on the perimeter of the town. Is the land located where the action is? Is it in the right area of town?

Public utility companies are a good source of growth information, because their planning is made in advance of population growth.

The analyst should also talk with community action groups and even with local citizens to learn how people in the area would react to further development and whether the buyer should anticipate opposition from any organized groups.

Bruce Nott is a firm believer in talking with the average local citizen to really find out about a piece of property:

What might look to an outsider to be a really superior piece of property might have a problem connected with it that only 10% or 20% of the local people know. They know which direction the wind blows from the dump; whether or not there is a serious drainage problem; whether there is serious traffic congestion in the vicinity; the quality of and any problems with the schools; if there is a problem with noise pollution, either from autos and trucks, airplanes or factories, and any problem that might not readily be apparent. In seeking out land, you're not going to find out all of these things until you've been in negotiation, maybe even opened escrow, or signed a contract and had money change hands. Then you realize this particular piece of property is sold every year to an outside developer who takes an option on it and it is a perpetual option piece.

The local chamber of commerce and industrial development commissions are excellent sources of quantitative statistical information. The analyst's job is to put everything in the proper perspective.

QUANTITATIVE ANALYSIS

William E. Becker's organization uses a comprehensive land acquisition checklist and report form to prepare reports for clients in connection with the purchase of land. In addition, the checklist is employed in site feasibility and utilization when the firm is asked to answer "What is the highest and best use for the property?"

Becker warns that the checklist is only as good and reliable as the researcher who prepares it or any part of it, and this must be weighed by the consultant prior to any recommendation to a client.

Some of the information called for in the Becker checklist follows.

Ownership. Name, address, and telephone number of the owner.

Land. Location; legal description; city or county; whether annexable; gross and net size as well as lot size; frontage, depth, and shape.

Improvements. Description of any improvements, including approximate dollar value and condition; whether income-producing; if so, amount of income produced and cost of removing improvements.

Lease. If the land is leased, what is the present term, amount, and percentage? How can the lease be terminated? When?

Referral. How was the land found? By a broker, newspaper ad, or sign? If by a broker, his name, firm, address, and telephone number. Is a commission payable? If so, by whom and how much? Will the broker cooperate, can the commission be deferred, and can the broker deliver? Is the listing an open, exclusive, or term?

Owner. Does the owner want to sell? Where is he employed, and what is his position? What kind of person is the owner? Is there proof of ownership? Has this been verified? If so, how and when?

Asking Price.   How much total cash down payment is required per acre, per lot? Terms in years, interest percentage, and details.

Title.   Who pays? Is there proof in the form of an abstract or title insurance? What is the name, address, and telephone number of the title company, the name of its representative, and the cost? Is a binder available?

Does any material exception encumber its marketability? If so, what is it?

Are there any unrecorded easements? If so, describe whether squatters' rights or restrictions in building height, size, set back, lot size, family size, color, or architectural style, or some other requirement. When recording restriction, the location, book number, page number, and date should be listed. Are the restrictions amendable? If so, how? Who can amend them and when?

Existing Real Estate Tax Assessments on Improvements.   On paving, sewerage, water, pump station, lights, and other assessments, how much is the periodic payment? When and for how long is it made? What is the total amount? Are these specials assumable or must they be paid by the seller?

Existing Liens.   What is the existing principal balance on the first mortgage, trust deed, or land contract? To whom are payments to be made? Are they monthly, quarterly, semiannual, or annual? How much is each installment and what is the interest rate? Is the interest to be paid in addition to the principal, to be included in the amount of the fixed installment, or to be paid by another method?

Are any balloon payments required in the future? Can the lien be assumed? Can the balance be prepaid without penalty? Can the lien be subordinated to construction loans? Does the lien provide partial releases? If so, on what basis? Who is the mortgagee? Does the mortgage contain any onerous provisions a buyer might not want to assume? The same information must be completed for second mortgage, as well as for any other existing liens.

New Liens to Be Used as Instruments of Financing.   What is the principal amount of indebtedness for a new mortgage or a purchase money trust deed? To whom are the payments to be made to and when? What is the amount of the installment? The rate of interest? Is the interest to be paid in addition to the principal, to be included in the amount of fixed installment, or to be paid by another method?

Are any balloon payments required in the future? Can the mortgage be assumed by a subsequent buyer? Can the mortgage be subordinated to construction loans? Can portions of the land be released without full payment? If so, on what basis? Has the proposed mortgage form been reviewed? Should any provisions be stricken? Similar information is necessary if the new land contract is a contract for the deed. The analyst also considers other methods or instruments of financing.

Escrow. The name, address, and telephone number of the escrow agent, officer, date of opening. The duration of escrow, and how the fee is to be split between buyer and seller. The name, address, and telephone number of the attorney selected.

Contingency clauses in escrow instruction should include: approval of title report by buyer; availability of utilities; approval of map by city or county; buyer's approval of soil report; buyer's approval of engineering study; approval of zone change by city or county; approval of financing, term, and others as may be determined.

Liens (other than existing mortgage liens). Mechanic's, materialmen, tax, or judgment? Are liens to be cleared by the seller prior to closing the transaction?

Easements and Rights of Way. What are the public utilities easements? Are there any other easements? If so, describe them. Is there any private or public right of way? Can certain harmful easements be cleared prior to close of escrow?

Survey Information. Has the land been surveyed? If so, when? List the name, address, and telephone number of the surveyor. Is the plat available? Are the boundaries staked? Are exact boundary lines known? What are the uncertainties? Will the neighbors cooperate in settling boundaries? Will the seller bear the expense of settling boundaries?

Physical Analysis of Land. Altitude and topographical information on the degree and percent of the land that is level, rolling, sloping, and steep. Is the soil sandy, clay, loam, rocky, adobe, hard caliche, soft caliche, alkali, saline, or other?

Are soil test reports available? If so, have they been ordered? When were these reports made? By whom (name, address, and telephone number)? Summary of soil report(s). Will soil conditions necessitate excessive building costs?

Is a copy of a U.S. Geodetic Survey topographic map available? Are there any apparent topographic problems? Are drainage and flood data available from the U.S. Army Corps of Engineers?

What is the climate of the area?

What percent of the land might be considered lost due to vertical slopes, underwater (swamp), deep gorges or washes, floodcontrol easements, utility easements, and other problems or easements?

Is vegetation growth light, moderate, or heavy? Is the existing vegetation a help or a hindrance? Is there any marketable timber? If so, how much and what type of trees?

Can the mineral rights be purchased with the land? Gas and oil rights? Other rights? Will the holder of rights quit-claim? Will the holder of rights quit-claim surface entry and the first 500 feet? Who pays for clearing rights?

Does the land have any natural or man-made bodies of water, such as streams, lakes, ponds, river, or ocean frontage? What is the amount of water frontage? Does the water run year-round? What would happen in a dry spell?

Are there groves on the land? If so, what kind? What were the annual income and expenses last year? The two previous years? Who farms the existing crop? When was it planted?

Has the farmer given written release of tenants' rights? Does the farmer plan to continue farming or does the seller require that the buyer farm until he is paid? Does the existing trust deed require continued farming? Can trees be burned or do smog control regulations forbid burning.

Does the land have any outstanding attributes, such as waterfront lot potential, ocean view, or mountain slope view lots? Is there potential for a retirement community? Are adequate hospital facilities and practicing medical doctors nearby? How many and how far away are they? What are the names of the medical clinics and hospitals in the area and their bed size? What is the proximity of parks and libraries; the names and sizes? Are there other community facilities? Is there a golf course? If so, is it private or public and what are the fees? What is its quality? Is membership available? The same data is needed for tennis courts, including clubs and numbers of courts.

Special Hazards and Nuisances. Check and explain if the land is characterized by or exposed to:

soil erosion   earthquake fault
heavy vehicular traffic   unusual air traffic
flight patterns   noise or vibration

explosives
smoke
other odors
flood hazard
unsightly views
dumping of junk/debris

fire
chemical fumes
poor surface drainage
high water table
TV interference

Accessibility.   What is the road distance in miles from a city and how large is its population? What is the road frontage of the land? Is the surface road black top, gravel, dirt, or some other surface? Is the road private, or is it a U.S. highway, state highway, county road, or city street? What is its size? Is the road lighted? Is traffic light, heavy, or moderate? Is it a commercial street or a truck route?

If it is a private road or if there is no road, is there a legally acceptable right of ingress and egress to the buyer? How much would it cost to acquire or improve access? Is the land accessible during all seasons of the year? Is a future freeway scheduled to be constructed through or near the land?

Public Use.   Is the land being considered for a park, school, freeway, or other public use? Is it under condemnation?

Transportation.   What is the nearest railroad station, long-distance bus terminal, or commercial airport (include name, frequency of service, and distance traveled). Is a bus or other transit system accessible to the parcel? If so, how far away does it stop? How frequent is the service? What is the fare? How long does it take to drive downtown? Are there any tolls on bridges or roads? How much are they? Are any new highways or freeways to be constructed within the next few years? If so, how close will they be to the property? How big will they be?

Utilities.   Is gas or electricity on the land? How close is the nearest gas line? What is the name of each utility? What promotional help will it give to a developer, and what is the cost?

Is water furnished by a public utility or by a private company? Is water on the land? How close is the nearest water line? What is the cost of running the water line? Are water costs refunded to the developer; if so, by what formula? Are any wells on the land? If so, what is the pumping depth, and what is the pumping depth of nearby wells? What is the estimated depth of ground water in the immediate area? Are there any reservoirs on the land?

Is there a sewer line on the land, or are sewage disposal facilities required in septic tanks (cesspools)? How close is the nearest sewer line? What is the cost of the sewer connection and fees to join the sewer district? Will·a pumping plant be needed to reach the sewer? At what cost?

Area Analysis.   Describe and photograph the nature of the surrounding land from the North, East, South, and West.

What is the name, address, and telephone number of the governing body? What services does it provide? What is the name and telephone number of the individual interviewed at the police, fire, and sheriff's departments?

How often is the trash picked up? By whom? Is this a union? What is the cost of the service?

Is the developer required to provide any municipal facilities or maintenance services?

Local Attitude Toward New Development.   What is the attitude of the governing body and of local citizens toward development? Check all relevant ordinances for subdivision, building, park dedication, underground utilities, and zoning. Are there any unusual or unduly expensive requirements?

Building Code.   Is there a uniform building code? Are there any unusual or unduly expensive local amendments? Can the buyer install his own utility systems? Would this be feasible and profitable? Does the governing body require subdivision bonds? Will it accept a lender's agreement in lieu of bond?

Nearby Facilities.   List the names, ages, and distances of neighborhood, local, and regional shopping centers with major tenants. Are any new facilities under construction or planned?

List the names, ages, distances, and sizes of the elementary school, junior high school, high school, college or university, and parochial or private schools. Is transportation available? Are new schools under construction or planned? List the names, denominations, ages, and distance of the churches in the area. Are any new churches planned?

A detailed list of recreational facilities should be made. Does the city require a donation of land for open space, parks, or recreation. What recreational facilities will be needed to be competitive? Will credit be granted toward open space requirements for such recreational facilities?

Nearby Residential Developments. List name, size, and type. How many developments have been completed in the last two years or are currently under construction within 15 miles, five miles, and one mile? What is the price range of the homes in the area? Where are the buyers coming from? Obtain similar information on older residential developments and the condition of the older homes. Is there market potential for move-ups from older homes? Are existing developments selling and why? What is the resale price range of homes in the area? Is the resale market strong or weak? What is/are the lot size, price, distance, and available utilities for residential lot subdivisions? Describe the competing tracts and competition from existing builders. Do existing builders work on adequate profit margins?

Nearby Apartment or Condominium Developments. Name, number of units, age, sale or rental rate per square foot, distance, basements, garages, carports, and type of resident.

Nearby Commercial and Industrial Developments. Commercial, heavy, medium, or light industry, age, distance, employees, and salary range. What is the employee turnover? What is the likelihood of increased employment in the next few years? Is any new industry planned or under construction? Type? Who? When?

Nearby Military or Government Installations. List with details; include effect of installations on the area's economy, particularly payroll impact.

Lenders. What do local and national lenders as well as other professional market researchers think about the market in the area, the specific price bracket for the land, and various types of planned improvements?

Local Contacts. List names, references, titles, positions, telephone contacts, and advice given by local title companies, banks, savings and loan associations, mortgage bankers, engineers, building departments, planning departments, and other sources.

Labor Availability. Is there an adequate number of subcontractors, suppliers, and workmen in the area? List the general contractors they have worked for; include photographs and map locations of projects.

Planning and Zoning Regulations. Present county, regional, city, or municipal zoning; include remarks concerning potential zoning change, who controls zoning, and any master plan for the area. Will there be resistance to rezoning from neighbors or the governing body? Is there local zoning apportionment?

Property Taxes. List annual taxes with assessor's valuation and on what percent of market value the tax rate for each $100 was based. How has the tax rate varied in the past five years? Is there a good tax base in the community now, with sufficient commercial and industrial property? List the name, address and telephone number of the county assessor. How can he be reached?

Subdivision Requirements. List anywhere applicable for state, county or regional, city or municipal, FHA, or VA.

Subdivision Process. List the basic steps necessary to obtain approved subdivision, and any other factors to be considered.

Subdivision Costs. Obtain best available estimates for the following:

engineering and surveying	soil tests
tree removal	structure removal
debris removal	moving water lines
removing defective soil	soil import
grading	drainage lines
curbs and gutters	sidewalks
street lights	street signs
trees	walls or fences
median island	special landscaping
park dedication	electricity
telephone	underground
gas	water
water connection fees	sewer
sewer connection fees	pumping plant
sanitation district	septic tank/cesspools
off-tract costs for water	bond premium
off-tract costs for sewer	superintendence
other off-tract costs	inspection fees
interest	property taxes
overhead	miscellaneous

Estimate the total subdivision costs, total raw land cost, and number of raw and finished lots.

Value Analysis. Compare the price per acre (or lot or front foot) with similar land offered for sale or recently sold in the area. Is the land more or less expensive? By how much, and what is the reason? What is the potential use for the land in three to five years, five to ten years, and more than ten years? Is developmental growth spreading in the direction of the land, and how far away is it at present? What is the estimated time it will take development to reach this general area? Is the price of the land low enough to appreciate from the effects of inflation or speculative interest alone?

Comparables on Past Sales. What did this land or comparable land sell for one year, three years, and five years ago? Are there indications that the price trend will continue upward, level off, or turn downward? If the trend is up, is the rate of increase even, slower, or faster? How long can the buyer afford to hold the land? One to three, three to five, five-to-seven, or more than seven years?

What should the client's objective selling price be? How does research affect the outlook for realizing this objective selling price in the alloted time? Should the client buy the land? Why? Is a partner needed? What is the size of the profit potential?

Does the client intend to use any or all of the land for his own purposes? How much, and in what manner? Are there tax advantages connected with the land? Are there deductions for interest and property tax, depreciation of trees, buildings, and equipment, removal of trees, sale as a capital asset, or other deductions?

Is the land reasonably priced? Are the terms and price subject to negotiation? What terms and price should be offered?

List the outstanding reasons for buying the land.

List the outstanding reasons for not buying the land.

Name of researcher (signed) and date.

In addition, the buyer needs to know his cash requirements at closing, including principal, prepaid interest, management fees (if any), estimated taxes, closing costs, legal fees, insurance, and accounting. It is important that the buyer know how many years and months he will pay only interest and how many years he has to pay back the principal. The buyer should ·determine if the property is to be purchased with a wrap-around note. If so, he should know the ramifications of such a note. The buyer should be aware if there is a penalty for prepaying the outstanding balance of the note and if prepayments of principal apply to the next maturing installment of the note or to the end of the note.

It is important to obtain good legal and tax advice as to the amount of invested cash that is tax deductible for the entire interest-only period and for each year until the principal is paid. Tax laws change, so this is necessary when carrying land that has been purchased. There are many good attorneys and accountants, but the buyer should choose an advisor who is extremely knowledgeable and experienced in real estate. No one would go to an ophthalmologist or gynecologist for open heart surgery. The same degree of specialty is required for real estate transactions.

Depending on the client's requirements, the consultant may also either recommend or retain other specialists to conduct various aspects of the research, including geologists, surveyors, engineers, and land planners.

QUALITATIVE ANALYSIS

Quantitative research is just one part of the total process of land evaluation. The consultant must analyze each piece of information accordingly and draw on his own professional experience and knowledge to make his recommendations.

Architect Robert Martin Engelbrecht of Princeton, N.J., believes a current trend is developing that places critical emphasis on being assured of power or utilities rather than on approval of a project by the zoning officer or building inspector. Engelbrecht explains:

You've got your utility authorities acting almost independently of the government agencies in many areas.

Historically, we've always thought we could overcome problems and that as people we could go in, buy land, and exercise the great American ingenuity to make it work. Quite often, we have made it work after the fact.

In one area, a power company would not run the utilities seven miles to a new project. They wanted nearly $300,000 to bring in power. After reviewing the feasibility studies, we recommended our client build his own power plant. The costs of the total energy plant were equal to those of the public utility company. Ideally, it is better to let the utility company come in, because of operational problems. Once the utility was notified it would not be needed, that we were going to build our own plant, they then put in the power lines without any charge.

In a similar case, a local government required the developer of another project to spend considerable money to extend a water main to the property. Our studies proved we had ample water on the site and could dig our own wells. Establishing our own water company would be less than the cost of extending the main. Once the local utility was confronted with this, they decided to share the cost with the developer rather than lose the immediate and future business from the new location of the main.

In both cases, once an alternate plan was found, the utilities, who look to continuous flow revenues, were so advised that they decided a compromise was much better than the potential loss of the income that would be derived. The roles simply reversed.

Irwin Adler prefers to meet with local political leaders to get a personal feeling of their attitudes toward development. "We're very sensitive to the ecological, environmental, and no-growth feeling in a community. We walk into the city, county, or municipality we might be doing business with and tell them what we want and that we want to know up front if there are going to be any problems. We want to know the political structure now rather than get surprised with a fight later."

Richard W. O'Neill, who heads the Housing Advisory Council, Ltd., in Lakeville, Connecticut, claims ignorance of the marketplace, rather than stupidity, is one of the major reasons for failures in the building business caused by large inventories in 1974 and 1975.

"Demographic and economic variables tend to indicate the economic health and market strength of various comparable and competing cities and counties. From a large number of variables, which tend to indicate the economic strength of a metropolitan area and an opportunity for construction, indicators should be selected which have a minimal degree of redundancy and which depend on an easily obtainable data base. Because the variables are relatively more or less powerful in indicating potential opportunity, they have to be weighed," he says.

O'Neill includes these variables, which he qualitatively evaluates, in a list of 150 checkpoints. He looks for absolute population change in the most recent decade and half-decade periods and for percentage population and projections for the same five- and ten-year periods. O'Neill also determines population distribution by age group in Standard Metropolitan Statistical Areas (SMSAs) in categories of 15-25, 25-34, 35-54, and 55 and over.

Personal and household incomes in prior years and changes in the unemployment rate and the distribution of employment by industry are also important. O'Neill states:

The viability of any market depends on the diversity of its industrial and commercial base and its general employment levels. Consistently good growth areas with low unemployment rates usually are found in cities with a diversified employment base.

Cities with the most diversified economies are ones usually judged to be most recession or depression proof. The measure taken is the "Index of Specialization," the lower the figure meaning the more diverse the economy. The determinant is the number of people in job classifications, including manufacturing nondurable goods, manufacturing durable goods, agriculture and mining, contract construction, transportation/communications/utilities, wholesale and retail, financial/insurance/real estate, services, and government. A good balance will produce a low figure and a lack of balance, a high figure.

O'Neill points out that in 1975 Nashville had an Index of Specialization of under 2, whereas Las Vegas had an index of more than 12:

When comparing one city with another, the index of number of housing starts per thousand population directly and indirectly measures the strength of an economy and the opportunities in development activity. Directly, it shows that there are a lot of buyers and renters of new housing and that there is a strong and competitive housing industry. This is as important for a commercial and industrial developer as one involved in housing. Indirectly, it shows that the institutional constraints that a municipal or county government might impose on new building activity are not severe and that no-growth policies are not strong. It also shows that the sewage collection and treatment facilities are adequate at the present for projected urban growth over the next four years. You also can infer from that comparative figure that the union problem, which usually mitigates against new construction, is no big problem.

O'Neill also compares various communities and jurisdictions within an SMSA with regard to the real estate tax. He finds out if there are special and separate levies for schools, sewage disposal, water, parks, and street beautification, as well as what types of fees and whether land donations are required. With regard to local tax, O'Neill wants to know whether city management recommends that the city's dependency on property tax be reduced to absolutely the lowest level possible now that more equitable, responsive, and alternate sources of revenue are available, such as gross receipts, tax on utilities, sales taxes, user taxes, and revenue sharing. O'Neill tries to determine what actions the city or county is taking to change its tax structure, and especially if such changes would lighten real estate taxes.

O'Neill further evaluates current and projected municipal budgets, whether deficit or surplus, and the degree to which any deficits may affect general urban growth. "Various levels of expenditures for municipal services make one community more viable than another. Compare per-capita general revenue and direct general expenditure in local government finance with various other counties in the nation."

O'Neill also determines the bonding capacity of local governments and which municipalities have vetoed bond proposals, when, and for what reason. He believes the analyst also should know whether the state's bonding capacity is near its limit and whether trouble is pending over any "moral obligation" bond issues.

Business activity is measured and compared with other SMSAs to develop a business trend line using six indicators: employment, labor force, number of residential electric meters, taxable sales, adjusted value of building permits, and bank debits.

"You must get a reading on civic efforts to boost the industrial base and encourage business. These efforts can be very important to the general economic growth of an area, and the lack of same can do much to produce industrial flight. These efforts are not alone among chambers of commerce, but also involve the public sector at the municipal level through various agencies and appointed commissions. What is being done to attract industries? Is industrial financing available? Is there any effort to attract new service and capital goods industries?"

O'Neill believes that land-use controls, exercised by agencies other than those of local governments, should be increased in metropolitan areas. "They can affect what a developer may or may not do, sometimes profoundly, if he is not aware of the various directions in which such land-use agencies may move.

"The most common form of land control, outside of and sometimes over local government, is in the hands of councils of governments [COG] of various jurisdictions. Find out if there is a council in the area and what its powers of advocacy and review are. Most COGs have approval powers over community-development, federal-grant requests before they are submitted to Washington. They retain these powers under federal revenue sharing."

According to O'Neill, councils of governments have two distinct disadvantages: they have no real jurisdiction over capital expenditures, and they are wildly nonrepresentative of a metropolitan area on a one-man, one-vote basis.

The researcher must be able to determine when "maybe" means "no," when "no comment" means "no," when a "no" is really a "no," and when a "yes" could be a "no." All this information must be quantified based on the researcher's judgment.

"I don't want an analyst to necessarily tell me I'm right," says Irwin Adler. "The problem is to get marketing insight into a market and justification for a course of action which will result in an adequate report. I need a devil's advocate. I want an opinion that is objective and not subjective. If I'm wrong, I want to know it, and why. If I'm right, I also want to know why."

Professional land research has saved companies and investors millions of dollars. However, one must always realize that no one is perfect; even the best can err.

CHAPTER III

LAND VALUATION

Land can be described as a tangible commodity but an intangible asset. Unlike stocks and bonds, traded commodities, and even foreign currency, the daily market value of land is uncertain and difficult to ascertain.

Stocks and bonds are traded on various exchanges, where at almost any time the price or value of a stock or bond can be quoted. This is also true for wheat, corn, pork bellies, plywood, precious metals, and other commodities for which not only current prices but prices for months ahead are readily attainable. Even the value of foreign currency is immediately available.

One really does not know what a particular parcel of land is worth, because land is sold so infrequently. Even when land is sold, the selling price may not reflect the *real* value of the land.

There are many methods of valuing land. The following terms require some discussion: assessed value, market value, and cost. Assessed valuation is of little significance when land value is reported on financial statements. Cost is the single most important factor in financial reporting. However, some important considerations (to be discussed later in this chapter) must be recognized relative to the appraised market value of a parcel of land.

Assessed value is the value placed on the land by a tax assessor. In most localities this amount is rather nominal, because vacant land normally is not valued at close to its market value or cost. Except in rare and unusual circumstances, tax assessors use a block approach, instead of making a careful analysis of each specific site. Therefore assessed value does not adequately indicate the true value of the property.

Market value is defined as the price a given property is expected to bring if it is sold on the open market, allowing a reasonable amount of time to find a buyer who knows all the uses to which the land is adapted and to which it is capable of being adapted. A fair market value can be determined by either a professional appraisal or an evaluation by the individual owner or the company's management that relates the land to values of comparable and adjacent or neighboring parcels. An appraisal by an independent professional, such as a member of the American Institute of Appraisers of the National Association of Real Estate Boards (MAI) or a Senior Real Estate Analyst or a Senior Real Property Appraiser member of the Society of Real Estate Appraisers (SRA), is frequently accepted.

Cost is the actual price paid for the land *plus* all acquisition costs, including title searches, escrow and other fees. Based on the accounting practices used, interest and taxes can be added to the cost of the land. These carrying charges may either be capitalized or expensed. When taxes and interest are capitalized or expensed. When taxes and interest are capitalized, they are added to the cost of the land annually until it is ready to be used or sold. When taxes and interest are expensed, they are treated as expense items in the year in which they were incurred.

CAPITALIZATION OF CARRYING COSTS

No rule has been promulgated by the accounting profession, but capitalizing interest and taxes is widely accepted in financial reporting within the real estate industry. In 1973, the American Institute of Certified Public Accountants, representing the opinion of its Committee on Land Development Companies, published accounting guidelines for retail land sales which were subsequently approved by the Accounting Principles Board.

The *AICPA Industry Accounting Guide for Retail Land Sales* specifically refers to capitalization of interest and taxes as an acceptable cost under certain conditions. Paragraph 51 of the guide states:

Costs directly related to inventories of unimproved land or to construction required to bring land and improvements to a salable condition are properly capitalizable until a salable condition is reached. Those costs would include interest, real estate taxes, and other direct costs incurred during the inventory and improvement periods. Interest is properly capitalizable if it results from (a) loans for which unimproved land or construction in progress is pledged as collateral, or (b) other loans if the proceeds are used for improvements or for acquiring unimproved land. The carrying amount of capitalized costs should not exceed net realizable value. Interest not meeting the above criteria, selling expenses (except those deferrable as previously indicated), and general and administrative expenses should be treated as expenses of the period in which incurred.

However, in June 1974, the Securities and Exchange Commission (SEC) seriously questioned the practice of capitalization of interest and began pressuring the accounting profession and public companies to no longer capitalize such costs but to expense them as incurred. Because SEC is more involved with the disclosure and regulation of public companies than with accounting principles, the method of accounting is outlined in the footnotes of the Commission's quarterly and annual reports.

A company may prepare financial statements that capitalize interest and taxes and still expense the carrying costs incurred for income tax purposes.

Here is an example of how land inventory can be illustrated on a captialized basis:

Year	Cost	Interest*	Taxes†
Dec. 31, 1972	$1,000,000	—	—
Dec. 31, 1973	1,170,000	$120,000	$50,000
Dec. 31, 1974	1,340,000	120,000	50,000
Dec. 31, 1975	1,510,000	120,000	50,000

* Interest was calculated at the rate of 12% per year.
† Taxes were calculated at the rate of 0.5% per year.

ONE ACCOUNTING RULE

In the accounting profession one primary rule is applied to financial statements: use cost or fair market value, *whichever is less.* Accountants do not distinguish between individuals, partnerships, corporations, and privately or publicly held entities. The only practical difference this rule defines is that the individual or nonpublic entity has greater freedom to informally present data that do not normally conform to the accounting rules or regulations of SEC.

A public company can never value its land assets at more than cost, and always must write down or devalue its land holdings if the fair market value falls below cost. It is widely accepted practice for individuals and private entities to prepare a balance sheet on a market-value basis when appreciated land values exist.

REPORTING BY PRIVATE ENTITIES AND INDIVIDUALS

An individual who prepares his own financial statement can usually be more flexible than most business entities in his reporting practices. However, unless the fair market values are supported by a professional appraisal, any lender should carefully scrutinize such statements, taking into consideration the past loan payoff performance, track record, and credibility of the individual.

Any certified public accountant preparing a financial statement for a private company or an individual will disclose market value if it is supported by an intelligent, independent appraisal. Such valuation can be made parenthetically or in a footnote showing the effect on net worth in stating land holdings at fair market value. The disadvantage of this practice is that many lenders never read the footnotes. It is preferable to present the alternate value of the land in the body of the balance sheet. For example:

Land	Cost	Market Value
10 acres (corner of State Road 210 and Central)	$20,000	$36,000
Lot, 733 North Main	15,000	27,000

An even better way to present this information would be:

Land	Acquired	Cost	Market Value	Appraised
10 acres (corner of State Road 210 and Central, zoned R-1)	4/70	$20,000	$36,000	2/76, John Jones, MAI
Lot, 733 North Main (zoned C-2)	8/74	15,000	27,000	2/76, Joe Smith, SRA

The more information included in the financial statement to substantiate values, the more acceptable the statement is to a lender. If the financial statements have not been prepared in accordance with generally accepted accounting principles, the accountant's opinion must be stated.

"Lenders are becoming increasingly more sophisticated and astute in evaluating financial statements when market value is reported," says Kurt Alexander, a partner of Kenneth Leventhal & Company, Certified Public Accountants, Los Angeles. "Deferred income taxes arising from appreciated values should be reflected in a financial statement. Has the individual or private company set up a deferred tax liability for the tax that would be payable if indeed the land were sold at the expected profit? Many people ignore that to their dismay even when they look at their financial statements very closely. It often has a substantial effect on total net worth, depending on the tax bracket of the party in question. Lenders are most aware of such issues today."

According to Alexander, this disclosure can be made in an adjacent column or it can be footnoted. He suggests this entry:

Cost	Fair Market Value
$1,000,000	$2,000,000
Deferred Tax	$500,000

Thus the addition to net worth resulting from appreciation is $500,000 (the appraisal increment of $1,000,000 *less* a related tax of $500,000, which is deferred to the future).

REPORTING BY PUBLIC COMPANIES

Whenever land is valued at less than cost, a common occurrence during down cycles and recessions in the real estate industry, the company must revalue its assets and reduce the cost basis of the land. Deterioration of land values has been a significant factor for land oriented real estate companies reporting losses in recent financial periods.

Once land has been revalued on the books its value can never increase above that figure, even if an appraisal by an independent professional discloses that it is actually worth two, three, or even ten times its stated value. On the other hand, land assets can be recorded any number of times as the value of the land drops. If the land is sold at a higher value, then the difference is reported as profit.

If there are significant increases in value over cost, Kurt Alexander believes that a company has the responsibility to disclose this information. "Investors may be misled as to the value of the company's stock if there were no disclosure," says Alexander. "It is just a matter of properly informing its shareholders and potential investors so they can make intelligent decisions. If properties of a company in which I own stock or am interested in acquiring stock have a lot more value than is appearing on its balance sheets, I want to know about it."

Similarly, the company can go beyond the restrictions normally applied to financial reporting and include such information in the text of its reports to shareholders. If land value increases are significant, they should be referred to in the president's letter or whatever general information is written about the company.

OTHER FACTORS AFFECTING VALUES

Professional appraisals of land are becoming more and more difficult because of the sudden moratoriums being imposed on development, the volatile impact of environmental considerations and zoning and density rollbacks, and the influence of no-growth advocates and fluctuating political bodies. Real estate is a cyclical business, and land valuation rises and falls. When economic factors cause the value of many assets, particularly land holdings, to decline more than the value of the currency, one is faced with the basic question of whether land indeed has sustained its value, even with double-digit inflation. During any economic cycle, the businessman and his accountant must face the problem of questioning the value of land assets. Where an investor, speculator, or company can almost certainly expect land values to appreciate a certain percentage each year, the x factor of currency devaluation must be continually reweighed and reevaluated.

CHAPTER IV

ENTITIES OF ACQUISITION AND SALE

Many entities normally acquire and sell land, but the most common are individuals, partnerships, trusts, and corporations. Deciding which entity or combination of entities to employ to acquire land is influenced by such factors as taxation of potential profits, classification of the owner as a developer, and limitation of financial liabilities.

Prior to making a decision regarding the use of the various entities, the objectives and goals of an individual land-holding transaction should be carefully outlined and the final decision should be guided by consultation with competent legal and accounting professionals. One should not assume that experience in land acquisition alone, however extensive, is a sufficient qualification in forming the acquiring entity.

Changes in tax laws, the method of offering partnership interests, and local laws regarding the real estate trust are only three of the many ever-changing factors that are best known to the accountant and the legal counselor.

INDIVIDUALS

The simplest form of land acquiring entity is the individual. This may be one person or a husband and wife. The transaction can be deeded to husband and wife, tenants in common, or joint tenants. Some states require an individual to be identified as unmarried on any title. Laws vary from state to state as to how married persons can buy and sell land and whether one or two signatories are required for various parts of the transaction.

A company that is wholly owned by an individual and/or his or her spouse is considered a sole proprietorship. In general, this is considered an individual entity, whether or not the business is conducted under a fictitious name.

While acquisition by an individual is the simplest and most flexible way to acquire and sell land, the individual generally assumes total liability for the terms of the contract, notes, mortgages, and so on. In the event of default, he often faces the prospect of deficiency judgments and/or specific performance.

CORPORATIONS

A corporation can be privately or publicly held. Its stock can be owned by one or more individuals or other entities, or it can be wholly owned by or be a subsidiary of another corporation. State laws on corporate structure vary widely geographically.

Individuals, partnerships, or corporations normally engaged in real estate development often choose to establish separate corporate entities for individual land transactions. One of the most obvious disadvantages to acquiring property in a corporation is the prospect of paying both corporate taxes on the profit of the transaction and individual taxes on the distributed dividends. At times a Subchapter-S corporation can be established to avoid this problem of double taxation. The sale of a corporation's stock, as opposed to the sale of its asset, can often establish land-holding profits as a long-term capital gain to shareholders.

Jackson McDaniel cites an example of the structure of one such land transaction: "A large parcel of well-located land was available. The land was an excellent speculative investment, but my company could not take the burden of cash flow nor were we large enough to handle the entire development alone. Because of this, I established a separate corporation and sold stock to a very limited number of close financial associates. At the onset, we decided that the acquiring company would not develop the property and would take every precaution to avoid being classified as dealers or developers. As a corporation, we were able to do some third-party borrowing, which could not have been done by a limited partnership. We were able to qualify the profits as long-term capital gains by selling the entire corporation as opposed to the land as such," says McDaniel. However, he cautions that much of the advantage to such a transaction would have been lost if the corporation had sold land in various parcels and pocketed the profit as corporate income. "While there are some limitations to the Subchapter-S corporation, it could be used to avoid double taxation. I can think of no way where the cash distributed to the shareholders could be qualified for long-term capital gain treatment."

TRUSTS

The technique of acquiring property in a real estate trust (not to be confused with a real estate *investment* trust) is used extensively in the southwestern United States, but is not as common in other areas of the nation. McDaniel has used this type of entity to advantage:

In such a transaction, the seller deeds the land into a trust, and while he has relinquished title, the buyer does not hold that title. The interest of the seller (normally evidenced by a deed of trust or mortgage and note) is represented in the trust by a first beneficial interest. The buyer's interest is evidenced by a second beneficial in the trust.

The trustee, usually a bank, title insurance company, or trust company, holds fee title subject to an irrevocable and unconditional trust agreement. Such an arrangement has some obvious advantages for both parties. It is particularly advantageous when the sellers are a group of individuals with joint and undivided interest in the land. In the case of one trust, we acquired 400 acres jointly owned by 22 individuals with equal and undivided interest in the property. By deeding the land into trust and establishing irrevocable trust instructions, there was no further need to obtain the signatures of the individual sellers for such matters as partial reconveyance, signing of plat-maps, or zoning applications. It is obvious that such a trust must be drawn in great detail, because the trustee can act only on the instructions as they exist in the trust agreement.

The advantage to a seller, as well as to a buyer, is that a trust insulates the title against insolvency, bankruptcy, probation of estates, and personal or financial liabilities of the buyer and seller.

If the title is placed in trust subject to existing liens, it is desirable, though maybe not normally legally mandatory, that the lien holder be advised and concur in the transfer of title to the trust.

Generally, lenders will take a collateral assignment of the buyer's beneficial interest in the trust as security for land-improvement loans. The buyer has the advantage of holding the land subject to a purchase money mortgage. The improvement lender feels secure, because he knows that if anything goes wrong and he has to execute his collateral assignment, he is in the same position as if he had made his loan in the conventional manner. Additionally, as long as he meets the terms of the trust, he does not have the problem of having to renegotiate with the purchase money mortgage holder and is protected from any possible foreclosure or other actions by the seller.

The structure of trusts used in Mexico is discussed in detail in Chapter XV.

PARTNERSHIPS

There are various forms of partnerships. Interest can be equal among all participants who share an undivided interest, or partners can participate to varying degrees with regard to ownership and income allocation.

General Partnership. In this form of ownership partners can have either an equally divided interest or a proportionate interest in the profit, loss, and liability of the partnership, as specified contractually among the general partners. The general liabilities of either the general partnership or the general partners in a limited partnership can be limited by contract with the seller.

Limited Partnership. In this form of ownership the investors are limited partners and have limited liability. The general partner normally assumes all liabilities. Syndicators commonly form limited partnerships. This is also a popular form of ownership when the parties know one another and when high income-earning investors consult a particular professional, who becomes the general partner. In such cases the general partner may also invest a cash amount equal to an investor's share and participate as a full partner. Because of the liability assumed, the general partner may receive additional compensation, but only after each investor has received his contributive share.

Joint Venture. A joint venture is a form of partnership. The interests can be equal, 51–49%, 60–40%, or any agreed-on division. A joint venture can be between an individual and a corporation, a corporation and a partnership, two corporations, or virtually any combination of entities. By carefully structuring the venture, one partner in a land-development joint venture can maintain an investor's posture and thereby preserve his long-term capital gain status. The establishment of such a joint venture requires careful analysis and formation and should be done only with the advice of a good real estate attorney.

Syndications. A syndicator is essentially a middleman who buys property, divides it into a limited partnership, and sells the interests to investors. Usually, the syndicator is the general partner and assumes all partnership liabilities. Syndication may be divided into specific property offerings and blind-pool offerings. In a *specific property offering,* the syndicator offers one specific parcel of land to investors. In a blind-pool offering, the syndicator raises the money before selecting a specific property. A syndication can be made by either private or public offering, depending on regulations that vary from state to state. Certain offerings must be registered with the Securities and Exchange Commission. The public sale of interests in a syndication exposes the syndicator, as the general partner, to possible suits under the securities laws by investors or regulatory agencies.

Land syndicates can be formed either for speculative growth or to produce income, depending on the objectives of the investor. Some syndicators employ a land-lease method, splitting the land from improved income-producing property. In such cases the building is syndicated and can be written off entirely over its useful life. The land can be syndicated to investors who wish to earn a guaranteed income from the lease income. The land can also be sold outright and then leased again at a guaranteed percent return plus participation in the sale of the building.

Abuses of land syndication were brought to light in Texas late in 1974. Many syndicators had not registered issues with any agencies and had made private offerings, adopting practices that were often illegal. In many states SEC or other state regulatory agencies provide reasonable safeguards for the investor, and no investor should rely solely on the statements of a syndicator. According to Ralph Shirley, individuals were general partners in several Texas syndicates and would create a new syndicate so one could sell to another at a profit. "It is nothing more than a pyramid club, and the last investor in will be the big loser."

Paul T. Pohly blames land syndicators for artificially increasing land values. "Investor partners pay 1990 values for land purchased in 1975, with no chance to profit except by selling to a greater fool. There is no question about the financial appreciation capabilities inherent in land acquisition. The only true and dependable value is the price an eventual user can afford to pay for the land."

The most important consideration in investing in any limited partnership, regardless of its size, is the reputation, performance, reliability, honesty, integrity, and financial stability of the general partner.

Harry Kwartler advises that limited partners be extremely knowledgeable, either through reputation or personally, about their general partner. Kwartler also prefers to see limited partnerships formed among a handful of individuals, rather than several dozen investors: "Intimacy with the general partner and his integrity are vital, because the general partner can take his limited partners and drive them through the ground like a tent peg. It could be a nightmare."

Mutual Land Clubs. This form of partnership is similar to a mutual investment club. According to Robert Martin Engelbrecht, mutual land clubs are not new:

The first time I became involved with a club was in the late 1950s, with a group of five cliff dwellers in New York City who had bought a 40-acre farm in New Jersey. They wanted a master plan for the property and decided to go with undivided interests. The individuals had planned to select locations for summer homes for their own use, and the plan was accepted by the local township.

Many people in such clubs will buy land for cash. The only carrying cost they have in mind is taxes. Land in this country has had a guaranteed 5% appreciation per year, regardless of where it was. It didn't always appreciate 5% that one year, but somewhere in the cycle of five, ten, or 20 years, it has averaged out to at least 5% appreciation.

There are roots associated with investing in land. It is tangible. Large parcels of land have a better chance of appreciating than small parcels. Larger parcels can be bought at a much lower per unit cost, as a general rule.

One of the faults of mutual land clubs is the fact that, as individuals, they don't have the time to find land at a reasonable value or a timetable for development. They haven't sought out good professional advice.

Engelbrecht cites how mutual land clubs can function virtually as an investment group for land brokers and developers, using a formula similar to an equal general partnership. "A New Jersey broker did not have the cash reserves to accumulate land on his own, so he started a club with a dozen or so high income-earning professionals. The broker acts as the catalyst for the holdings. Land is bought with a renewable option each year. The parcels are bought for the personal use of investors. The parcels are strictly investments. They are never bought in a prime tax area. They are bought for long-term cycles of ten years, with the profitable gains being taxed as capital gains."

SEEK THE BEST AVAILABLE ADVICE

Corporate laws change. Tax laws change. State tax and corporate laws vary geographically. What worked successfully at one time in one state may not work successfully in another state or even in the same state in another year. Before structuring the land acquiring entity, the investor should be sure that all participants have obtained the advice and counsel of a reputable real estate attorney and accountant.

CHAPTER V

LAND-ACQUISITION
TECHNIQUES

Buying land is not like buying anything else. The terms, conditions, sale price, and method and time of payment are virtually whatever is agreed on by the parties involved in the transaction.

The buyer must consider the interests of the seller. Contractual consideration also must be given to when the land may be improved or developed. Is the buyer holding the land for investment and resale at a later date? Or is the land to be immediately developed?

Two land acquisition agreements are rarely alike. Clauses in the agreements vary according to circumstances, such as tax consequences of the seller, economic conditions, supply of and demand for similar land parcels, available financing, and risks that might be assumed by either the buyer or the seller.

Acquisition agreements have become much more creative in recent years, because of the increasing risks and uncertainties inherent in development. Such risks are directly related to the increased demands of environmentalists and ecologists, to the vacillating nature so prevalent today in elected and appointed government officials, and to the procrastination and indecision of many government agencies.

If a builder or a developer must rely on a local government to rezone or to extend utilities, it is risky to be committed to buying the land. With layer on layer of government approval required today, it is wise for the buyer to include clauses that permit virtually any escape from the purchase. Terms can provide automatic extensions and can include or not include inflation clauses that would escalate the price of the land. Of course, such conditions would vary according to the demand for the property.

Even more than zoning, Lewis N. Wolff of the Wolff-Sesnon Development Company, Los Angeles, believes the most important key to development today is to have a building permit. In addition to unknowns, Wolff also cautions the buyer to consider the physical aspects of implementing development on the land.

Acquisition can be achieved through an option agreement or a purchase-money or earnest-money contract. A contract containing "subject to" or "contingency" clauses can be just as effective as an option, and many professionals in the real estate industry consider "option" a dirty word.

The Robert Martin Corporation uses a long-term contract that is basically an option, subject to obtaining a zoning change and the approval of all municipal and government authorities who have jurisdiction over the property.

"Years ago we would sign an option or contract to purchase a piece of land and would close title upon receiving all necessary approvals," says Martin S. Berger. "Today we have to keep the conditions in the deal even after the passage of title, or we delay the passage of title because of environmental considerations.

"A buyer must always consider the possibility of law-suits, even after zoning is approved. One could get all of the necessary government agency approvals, close the escrow, and then be subject to five years of delay, expense, and litigation because of a lawsuit from an environmentalist group."

PURCHASE PRICE AND DOWN PAYMENTS

The preferred way to buy land is with little or no cash, extended terms, and low interest rates. Of course, this is directly dependent on the economic conditions at the time of the negotiation.

Martin S. Berger believes that too often land buyers are overly sensitive to price:

I find that nonprofessionals in the land business focus on price per acre. If you do a careful economic analysis of the land purchase, you will find that price per acre probably is one of the least important factors that comes into the actual cost.

Sometimes it is cheaper in the long run to pay more for land on a per-acre basis. For example, take the case of a seller who is supersensitive to the price per acre. He has 100 acres and believes it is worth $12,000 an acre and that his land is worth $1.2 million. Trying to get him down to $10,000 an acre or a land sale of $1 million could be very wrong. Let the seller know you believe the price may be high, but that you are willing to meet that price provided he agrees to certain terms and conditions. Then you are in a position to negotiate lower interest rates, better terms, and include a long list of conditions that otherwise would not have been possible with an unhappy seller who believes you would be stealing the land from him at the lesser price.

David Riese believes that the whole terminology of buying and selling has changed in recent years and now contains less references to "price per acre" and more terms related to "price per buildable unit." "An acre of apartment land today really doesn't mean much. What does count is the number of units that can be built on the land, how high you can go, and the parking requirements," Riese states.

When he wishes to begin immediate construction on the land to be acquired, Riese includes a clause in the land acquisition contract that requires building permits to be issued before the sale closes. "I want permits in my hand that allow me to build the project, and I will pay a higher entry price to acquire that right."

William Becker goes even further than Riese. "We do not recommend our clients close escrow and take title until after construction has started. We may pay $10,000 for an option and make a payment of $150,000 when we get the building permits. Sixty days later we may pay another $200,000 and have the property then released in stages."

Initial payments with an offer or contract can be made in various forms other than cash, including stocks, bonds, warrants, stock options, or even tax-free municipal bonds. For example, a seller may be satisfied with a municipal or a government bond that has a face value of $10,000 but a market value of perhaps only $7500. A seller may accept this bond as an initial payment based on its par value, if he is permitted to keep the interest the bond earns during the contingency period.

Sometimes Ralph Shirley uses a letter of credit. "Certain states prohibit title or escrow companies from paying interest on deposits. I have the title company buy a certificate of deposit for me at my bank with my earnest money. The title company still controls the deposit, but I receive interest on the money during the escrow period. Many unsophisticated buyers don't realize they can keep their money working to continue earning money," Shirley says.

A sophisticated owner probably would not want a deposit or funds released out of escrow until the sale of the land is final. Depending on the contract and local laws, an unscrupulous buyer could commit the owner for an indefinite period of time once the seller accepts a deposit outside of escrow.

MORATORIUM CLAUSES

Attorney David Clurman of the New York law firm of Phillips, Nizer, Benjamin, Krim & Ballon suggests that the buyer place a moratorium clause in any transaction when land is purchased for development.

"Such a clause should provide that no installments or interest payments shall be due and payable during any period of time that any government agency has taken any action to bar the development of various types of housing or other intended uses of the land involved," advises Clurman. "In addition, the clause should provide for a moratorium on such payments while any court or administrative injunction or order is outstanding that bars such usage, where instituted by a government agency, citizens' group, public-interest association, surrounding residents, or others.

RELEASE CLAUSES

Release clauses should be clearly defined in any transaction involving a sequential acquisition of land. Lewis N. Wolff believes a buyer who is planning to develop the land should estimate his own development program in as much detail as possible, have his concept clearly approved by the seller, and, if possible, attach an exhibit pertaining to the release clauses desired. Wolff elaborates:

A tract map, as an example, may have the land divided into say 12 parcels for sequential acquisition. The program may start with the release of parcel #1 in the northwest corner and then parcel #2 adjacent to it. However, the local municipality then may require a sewage treatment facility on the site which is proposed for parcel #12, located in the southeast corner, most distant from the first parcels. To put such a facility on existing land that has been released could destroy its value as well as not be acceptable to the municipality or the company as part of its master plan.

Such contingencies must be carefully spelled out in the program regarding sequential release of parcels as related to the development process. This is vitally important for the success of the project.

EXCULPATION CLAUSES

Few sophisticated land buyers execute a contract without an exculpatory clause to protect themselves from any personal liability. This is an agreement between seller and buyer that the only security for the mortgage is the real estate itself. A typical exculpatory clause might read:

The owners and holders of said note agree to look only to the property securing same for the recovery on any obligations set forth in said notes. And in no event shall an action in the nature of a deficiency judgment be filed or prosecuted against the maker(s) of the notes, but the holders of such note or notes shall look exclusively to the security for the payment of all sums, including principal, interest, and all attorney's fees, payable or to become payable under the terms of this note.

Harry Kwartler has a good argument for a seller who balks at an exculpatory clause. "If the land owner says, "Hold it! You mean you're not going to personally guarantee the mortgage?" I respond that we bought a $1 million piece of land with $200,000 down and the mortgage is only $800,000.

"I point out to the owner that if an $800,000 purchase-money mortgage is insufficient collateral for the property, then in effect he is telling me that the land is not worth even $800,000, and we were fools to have paid as much as $1 million. If the seller suggests that he has an insecure mortgage, my posture is that the land is not worth the price we are paying. This is an almost irrefutable argument," he believes.

SUBORDINATION

Land subordination was once commonplace. Richard L. Weiss believes that in light of current protracted municipal processing, this practice will again become popular. Subordination keeps the owner involved, requiring him to subordinate his interest in the land to a construction mortgage or other prior lien.

Land can be acquired with a purchase-money contract through subordination. When the builder is paid at the closing of the escrow of a sales house, he then pays the seller of the land. Until that happens, the seller's mortgage becomes a second mortgage to the construction loan.

"Subordination usually is not practical except where sales housing is involved, because otherwise there is no subsequent sale escrow closing to provide payment to the seller," Weiss says. "However, there are ways the seller can subordinate his interest and become a partner in an income-property project.

"Subordination can be the ultimate in land acquisition, because it is a means of controlling land with a minimum of cash or other form of payment.

In almost half of Bruce Nott's land-development transactions in the last five years the land has been subordinated in some way. But Nott warns that subordination does not do that much good unless the money deferred is more attractive than the money that can be borrowed. "In other words if you buy a piece of property for $1 million and the owner agrees to subordinate, you must be able to borrow the money on terms from him cheaper than you can from a lender, or it is not worth it."

Suggesting that the land seller remain in negotiation when the buyer feels that the seller may not be emotionally suited for it, is a purchasing technique used by Martin Berger. "During the negotiation on price or terms or conditions, we ask If you think the land is so valuable, then why don't you put it into the deal?" In most cases the seller has read or heard stories of people getting burned in real estate. He often quickly retreats to a more passive position. In his retreat, he usually sells his land cheaper with better terms."

ACCOMMODATING THE SELLER

Berger also believes that most landowners, whether they are small businessmen or farmers, are often overly sensitive to the tax consequences of a sale. He provides some sellers with basically free tax consultation and tries to point out sophisticated approaches to the sale of the land. Berger believes this helps to negotiate the transaction.

Semantics are important in any negotiation. The vocabulary and jargon used in the real estate industry may mean one thing to a professional and something entirely different to a typical seller. The choice of certain words creates certain feelings.

"Option" is a word Harry Kwartler never uses when talking to a farmer. "Ask him for a contract to purchase, with numerous contingencies in it," Kwartler suggests. "We use a contract with contingencies subject to certain events taking place which are to our benefit. We do not close until all contingencies are met."

Leverage is all important in any real estate transaction, and this is the ideal leverage situation, especially if the buyer has a refundable deposit.

"Annuity" is another word Kwartler uses frequently. "Annuity is an accepted word in the American psyche," he says. "The insurance companies have sold it for a long time. It creates the feeling of security and continuous payment. Refer to the purchase-money contract and the regular payments of interest and principal as required as annuities."

The extent to which some buyers will go to accommodate a seller is well illustrated in the following example. A developer assembling a large parcel of land in Florida needed a 30-acre piece fronting on a major road. In the course of the title search the buyer learned that the owner lived in California, was financially secure, had owned the land for more than 25 years, and had bought it on a whim when visiting a relative.

The property had been planted as a citrus grove, the owner had had someone else manage the property, and he had not seen it in the past 20 years. The owner had not considered selling the property. When first contacted he would not accept cash or a mortgage on the property. Trading a similar piece of property seemed the only inducement. Recognizing that he faced the problems in acquiring the property, the buyer reevaluated the need for the 30 acres and decided it was vital to the success of the project. It was a necessity.

The buyer negotiated with the owner and his tax advisor in the ensuing months. They agreed on a price and began considering properties, including ocean-front land in Florida, speculative condominiums in Hawaii, and land in California. Eventually, a gasoline station site adjacent to a freeway in California was purchased by the buyer and traded to the owner for the 30-acre parcel in Florida.

ACQUISITION WITH OPTION

Options can be exercised between sophisticated parties. Option payments vary according to the demand for the property in question. Option money is generally placed in an escrow account, where it may draw interest. If the option is not exercised, the buyer can recoup the interest on the deposit, but may be required to forfeit the option payment.

An example of how one buyer acquired land on an option basis follows. The parcel was 30 acres, with an option period of three years. The option purchase price was $300,000. The buyer closed the sale with a mortgage to the seller of $150,000 cash payable, $30,000 on the exercising of the option and $120,000 at the closing 90 days later. The balance of $150,000 was to be paid by a three-year, standing purchase-money mortgage, with a 9½% annual interest rate.

Releases of the land were at the rate of $12,000 per acre; ten acres released at the closing. All release payments were credited toward the amortization.

The buyer also included a subordination clause, so that from time to time the lessor subordinated to various construction and long-term loans. The lesser agreed to such subordination, with the conditions that all of the loans were institutional in nature, that the construction loans had a permanent financing commitment, and that all loans were for periods of not less than 20 years.

The mortgage of $150,000 was used to offset the down payment, and the seller charged a placement fee for the loan, with a 12% annual interest rate payable in equal monthly installments. The seller spun the loan off to a financier.

ROLLING OPTIONS

Another type of option is the rolling or rerolling option. A builder can option 1000 acres and immediately take title to 100 acres, with a remaining option on the balance of 900 acres. Under the terms of the agreement, the builder must take title to 100 acres each year, but the terms can overlap. The second 100 acres can be acquired in the third year, and the third 100 acres in the fourth year. The builder can take four years to pay for the 300 acres but not be obligated to a long-term purchase, because he has no carrying costs of interest and taxes and for a small fee up front controls the land by option.

THE CONTRACT PURCHASE

A purchase-money or an earnest-money contract is similar to an option. The fundamental differences are in terminology, not in substance.

All the contingencies that are contained in an option can be included in a fully documented purchase agreement, from which the seller cannot withdraw but the buyer can, if all the conditions of the agreement cannot be satisfied.

For large purchases of land, the purchase agreement can be structured in the same way as an option. For example, a buyer of 1000 acres can option the land, but a purchase-money contract can specify that title acquisition is to be restricted to 20% of the property in each of five consecutive years. The contract can provide continuing contingencies for each of the remaining parcels of land in the event the land is later down zoned or construction is delayed by any of several types of moratoriums. The seller is protected as well by an escalating scale for the sales price of the land, based on a cost-of-living index adjustment.

A zoning contingency can easily be added to a purchase-money contract. One buyer acquired 75 acres of one-acre zoned residential land for $335,000. The terms were an initial payment of $15,000 on signing the formal contract, with the money to be held in escrow in an interest-bearing account. An additional $35,000 was due at closing. The balance of the money due was to be paid by a purchase-money mortgage for a period of 10 years with 10% annual interest payable in semiannual installments. The principal payments of $30,000 per year commenced in the fifth year, with the balance due at closing. The buyer elected to divide the purchase-money mortgage into two sums, with 60% of the balance applicable to half the tract and 40% applicable to another portion of the tract. The releases were eight acres at closing and additional releases at the rate of $6000 per acre as needed for development.

The contingency was the fact that the property was to be developed as a 20-acre shopping center, and that the balance was to be used for garden apartments and townhouses. The buyer wanted six months to conduct the necessary engineering and market studies and to prepare drawings, plans, and other related documents to present before certain municipal bodies to obtain appropriate zoning for the proposed use of the land.

A clause in the contract stated that in the event such planning and application were in progress and had not been accepted, or in the event the buyer were filing suit against the municipality to gain approval for such zoning, then the contract could be extended for an additional six months at the buyer's option. The contract also stated that during the first six-month period, or the six-month extension, the buyer could notify the seller if he wished to discontinue efforts to obtain the property for land development. Then the contract would be canceled, and all deposits held in escrow would be returned to the buyer. Any interest earned on the deposit would be given to the seller, and the buyer would have to return all completed market studies and engineering regarding the land to the seller.

ACQUISITION AGREEMENT CHECKLIST

A checklist of the general criteria a buyer should consider including in a land-acquisition agreement follows.

A. Terms of the Contract

1. Seller pays for title policy assuring no title problems and guaranteeing deletion of area and boundary.

2. Purchaser pays for net acreage after deducting any easements, encroachments, and so on.

3. Seller pays for survey.

4. Taxes to be prorated at closing.

5. Seller pays legal fees for drafting the deed, note, and deed of trust. If possible, the buyer's attorney should prepare all documentation, but the seller may wish to set a dollar limit when paying the costs.

6. Purchaser should insist on specific performance on the part of The seller. However, The purchaser may legally limit his own specific performance, without invalidating the contract.

7. Contract should be subject to quasi-governmental approval, such as building permits, drainage permits, utility permits, flood-level approval, ingress/egress, major thoroughfare access, density, and so on.

8. If possible a minimum down payment should be made and the balance should be paid in 10–15 years, the first five years of which would be solely interest payments.

9. Seller may want to substitute a collateral clause for protection in the event of an early payoff.

10. Release clauses should be clearly outlined.

B. A Clean Title to the Property

1. No outstanding unknown liens or judgments.

2. No easements or encroachments.

3. No restrictions.

4. No zoning problems.

5. Control of 51% of the mineral rights, or total surface control.

6. No existing mineral leases.

7. No poachers or adverse possession.

8. Water rights if property adjoins a stream, river, or lake.

9. No assessments.

C. Development Privileges

1. Right to dedicate streets, utility easements, drainage easement, alleyways, and so on.

2. Utility district joinder clause.

3. Rights to zone or place deed restrictions.

4. Release privileges.

5. Subordination privileges, if possible.

D. Terms of the Note

1. Exculpatory clause for nonpersonal liability. The lien holder should only consider the land the security against the note.

2. Interest only payments for as many years as possible.

3. Prepayments for releases to apply against the next principal payments due.

4. No penalty for prepayment privileges.

5. All principal payments to apply as credit against releases, including the down payment if the seller agrees.

6. Moratorium clause to suspend payments during any action that delays development processes.

In preparing any legal documentation for an option or a purchase-money contract and in seeking counsel and advice prior to and during the negotiation, a buyer should retain a reputable legal counselor who is thoroughly experienced and knowledgeable in real estate law, particularly in the state in which the documentation is to be recorded.

CHAPTER VI

LEASING LAND

Land leasing is more a financing device than an acquiring device, but it does provide the user with a highly leveraged method of controlling the land for a specific period of time.

Leasing land is really no different than leasing automobiles or any other equipment. The lessor in effect provides the financing.

The major advantage of a lease is that the builder, developer, or investor never has to expend capital to buy the land, unless an option to buy is part of the agreement.

Land leases can be applied to virtually every type of real estate and are commonly used for industrial, commercial, and rental apartment projects. Land leases are not normally used for single-family residential sales properties, except in Hawaii, areas of southern California, and other select locations.

However, given the spiraling costs of home ownership and the ever-increasing significance of improved land as a great portion of total property cost, the concept of land leases for single-family housing may become more and more popular.

PHASING A LEASE

A land lease can be structured with options and even with options to buy. Terms can be specified in phase periods to give the developer time to accomplish his objectives. Generally, there are three periods in a phased lease. The initial term is for engineering and market studies. This is usually either the period of time before construction begins or a specified period of time (18 months, 24 months, or even 30 months), whichever is shorter. Construction can be defined as beginning when building permits are issued, when excavation begins, or when foundations are poured.

The time of the construction is the second phase of the lease, and the rent or lease payments on the land are increased accordingly. The final phase is the main-term rent, when development is complete and the property is in use. A main-term lease can range from as low as 6 times to as high as 12 or more times the capitalized value of the land, depending on the negotiated agreement.

During the initial phase of the lease, the owner normally pays for taxes and insurance. During the final phase, however, the user pays for taxes and insurance, so the lease payments are net to the lessor.

LEASE WITH OPTION TO BUY

Harry Kwartler believes the single best method of controlling a piece of property with the least amount of front money, excluding the one-dollar option, is to include a clause with an option to buy. For example, Kwartler structured a transaction with a land lease with an option to buy. The buyer wanted to tie up 40 acres (for garden apartments, with a density of 12 to the acre) on a 99-year lease, consisting of an initial term, a construction term, and a main term.

The initial term was defined as the phase during which all engineering and market surveys were to be completed (a maximum of 18 months). The construction term was to end when the buildings were erected and at least 90% occupied (again, a maximum of 18 months). The main term was to consist of the balance of the 99 years. The lease payment was $3000 per year for the initial term; $9000 per year for the construction term; and $25,000 per year for the main term. All rent for the land, with the exception of the initial term, was to be a net rent, payable in quarterly installments in advance.

The buyer added an option to purchase for the entire life of the lease, based on a purchase price of $280,000, with $20,000 to be paid on notice that the option is to be exercised and an additional $30,000 to be paid at the closing to take place 90 days later. The balance due would be paid by purchase-money mortgage for a period of 12 years at 10%

interest to be paid semiannually, with a principal of $20,000 per year on the sixth year and the balance due to be paid at maturity.

Releases of the land were to be contracted at the rate of $10,000 per acre, with 10 acres released at closing. All payments for amortization were to be credited toward the releases, and all payments of releases were to be credited toward the amortization.

On this particular transaction, the lessee requested the lessor to subordinate to various construction and long-term loans.

LEASE WITH OPTION TO BUY FOR INVESTMENT

In an economic period of increasing land values, Kwartler cites another example of a short-term lease with an option to buy that is highly leveraged for a speculative investor. The agreed-on land value was $1 million, and the rent was capitalized at 10%, or an annual land rent of $100,000. Whether or not the land is used, the buyer has acquired a $1 million piece of land with no money down, with a mortgage at 10%, and with an option to buy. In two years the value of the land increases to $1.2 million, and the option to purchase is worth $200,000 more. The buyer has paid $200,000 in rent and has realized an equal appreciation in value. The $200,000 rent is worth $100,000 to the 50% taxpayer, and the $200,000 appreciation is worth $140,000–150,000 to the capital-gains taxpayer. The buyer has made $40,000 on a $100,000 after-tax investment, which is a 40% (or an average of 20% per year) annual rate of return. If the appreciation were to continue over a five-year period it could be worth as much as $2 million. On the basis of an appreciation of $1 million, with the land doubling in value, the $500,000 land rent would be worth $250,000 to the 50% taxpayer in after-tax dollars. The land could be sold from a capital-gains position, realizing $650,000 after taxes.

THE SALE-LEASEBACK

The sale-leaseback is another technique that is basically a means of highly leveraged financing. An owner of both the land and improvement of income-producing property (such as a shopping center, rental apartment, motel, hotel, industrial park, or office complex) creates two forms of ownership: one for the improvement, and one for the land.

The land is sold and then released by the owner of the improvement, with an agreement over a specified period of time for a specified amount of rent. Ownership of the land lease can be an attractive investment for institutions or individuals seeking a high rate of return. The lease can produce an annual income of 10% or more, and there is an opportunity for equity appreciation by increasing valuation of the land. In some cases the new owner may receive a percentage of the net or gross revenues of the property.

The sale-leaseback of land under income-producing property is a creative technique for syndicators of tax-sheltered investments. The splitting of the improvement from the land is known as an A/B syndication. Part A is the improvement itself, which is sold to individuals seeking shelter. Part B is the land which is syndicated to individuals seeking income rather than shelter, with a guarantee of a set percentage rate of return.

The land tenant benefits not only from the depreciation of the improvement on the land, but his tax shelter from the land-rental payments increases as the gross income of the property increases. Thus it is usually practical for the owner of the improvement to employ straight-line depreciation and to keep the property at its maximum income-producing potential.

As land becomes more expensive and represents an even greater percentage of the total financing package, the sale-leaseback becomes proportionately more attractive. To achieve the best use of the sale-leaseback, the properties should provide a good income base and should show potential for increasing revenues.

The sale-leaseback is effective and useful when an owner of an existing project wishes to obtain cash from sale of the land rather than to refinance the project. The sale-leaseback also restores tax deductions on an older property on which much of the depreciation and shelter already has been used.

Lewis N. Wolff cautions that while a sale-leaseback is an effective means of obtaining cash, the developer must evaluate the effective cost of money to clearly see the bottom line. "While such a transaction can save hard dollars needed on front-end costs, the interest rate paid for the lease may result in less overall profit. Furthermore, you may have to give away some equity participation to make the transaction attractive to a partner. Generally, the combination rate of the land lease and the mortgage on the improvement will run significantly higher than the mortgage rate on the improvement and other forms of short-term borrowing, especially because the land will always be in a subordinate position to the first trust deed on the improvement," says Wolff.

RESIDENTIAL LAND LEASES

Selling single-family residential housing with long-term land leases is not a new concept, but it could be the answer to the problem of making housing affordable to the average American family.

In many areas of the country the cost of an improved lot on which to build a house is approaching the construction cost of the house itself. Some industry leaders predict that the cost of the land will eventually exceed the cost of the average house. In some of the more affluent neighborhoods, land value already exceeds the value of the improvement.

For example, consider a house that sells for $50,000, of which the construction cost (including marketing and sales cost and profit) is $30,000 and the value of the improved land is $20,000. Conventional financing would require a 20% cash down payment of $10,000, leaving a mortgage of $40,000. With a term of 30 years and an interest rate of $9\frac{1}{2}\%$, the monthly cost to amortize principal and interest would be $336.35.

On a land lease a 20% down payment on a $30,000 improvement for the same house would be $6000. Assuming that the land is capitalized at a rate of 8%, or an annual rent of $1600, the monthly cost to the homeowner would be:

$24,000 mortgage, 30 years, $9\frac{1}{2}\%$	$201.81
Land lease, 50 years, 8% cap rate	133.33
Total	$335.14

The monthly savings would be slightly more than $1, favoring the lease, but the owner would save significantly ($4000) on the down payment.

The figures become even more significant in a city or government project, such as one conducted by a redevelopment agency, where there is a need to provide decent housing for persons of low and moderate incomes, as well as those on fixed annual incomes. A government is in a position to totally subsidize the land, or to take less of a percentage of return on the land. The financing can be arranged through revenue bonds. Considering a $35,000 house in an urban development, the improved unit would cost $20,000; the land, $15,000. Based on a 95% loan-to-value ratio the owner would pay 5% down, or $1750. The monthly amortization of principal and interest on a 30-year mortgage for $33,250 at $9\frac{1}{2}\%$ interest would be $279.61.

The owner would pay only $1000 down to lease the land, and the city could afford to capitalize the land value of $15,000 at 6%. The figures would then be dramatically different:

$19,000 mortgage, 30 years, 9½%	$159.77
Land lease, 50 years, 6% cap rate	75.00
Total	$234.77

Thus the owner is afforded a monthly savings of $44.84 and $750 of the cash down payment.

The savings would be even greater for inner-city housing if the local government were to totally subsidize the land cost, or if state and federal funds were used to piggyback the subsidy of the land and the residential unit.

Various government agencies could work together to provide incentives to encourage builders from the private sector to return to the inner city. Local governments are in a position to offer land that is already zoned, with all approvals and environmental impact reports, so that once the builder has negotiated successfully with the city, he can immediately begin to build and sell the units. City officials are in a better position to expedite approvals than the builder working alone without their cooperation.

Deducting the land cost from the total financing cost of the unit almost immediately places affordable housing within the reach of millions of American families who are currently priced out of the market. This concept, even when applied as an indirect subsidy of a local government, still permits the private sector to be involved in the development process, and the contribution of funding needed by a government can be more readily predetermined.

Richard L. Weiss believes it is most difficult to sell to the prospective homeowner. "There is a genuine reluctance on the part of most purchasers of residences to leasehold interests. While there should not be from an economic viewpoint, there is a definite psychological impediment," he says.

In 1959 Weiss leased land from Indians in Palm Springs for residential development because Indians were prohibited by restrictive covenants from selling the land. The improvements were sold, and the homeowner signed a long-term lease for the land.

"Land leases can represent significant cost savings for residential development, but the consumer, the government, and lending institutions first must be educated," says Weiss. "The opportunities are there that benefit all involved in the project. The developer also may benefit by reducing the total price by an amount less than the actual cost of the improved land, thereby picking up on the front end an additional increment of profit."

A number of financial institutions became large landowners during the real estate crash of 1974–1975. These savings and loan associations, commercial banks, and insurance companies are now in a position to become the land lessors of the future. They already understand the actuarial process and can readily determine the capitalization rate needed to realize a profit. The lenders could also sell such projects to various institutional investors, such as pension funds, who wish to diversify investment portfolios with a greater percentage of fixed income investments.

THE LEASE AGREEMENT

The form and substance of the lease agreement is similar to that of a purchase-money contract. However, Bruce Nott cautions that at the outset both parties must thoroughly understand the relationship and all pertinent facts about the project. "You're going to be wed to that landlord for the term of the lease, and you must make certain that your landlord is practically as familiar with the project as you are when you start," Nott advises.

In addition to the key points in the purchase-money contract, the basic differences that must be considered when using the land lease include:

1. An option to purchase at a specified time.

2. The capitalized rate of the value, or the amount of the annual rent.

3. How the rent will be paid: monthly, quarterly, semiannually, or annually.

4. Escalation clauses based on a fixed amount, cost-of-living index, currency valuation, or other factors.

5. Who pays the taxes and insurance, and when (if there are phases to the lease).

6. Right of assignment of the lease.

7. The purchase price (if there is an option agreement), or a formula to use to determine the purchase price, with the terms and conditions of the purchase so outlined and defined, including financing or participation by the lessor.

8. Additional rent incentives that might be considered for various types of commercial, income-producing properties.

9. Definitions of the various phases of the lease (predevelopment, development or construction, and main term).

10. Conditions for razing improvements on the land.

11. Options for lease renewals.

CHAPTER VII

FINANCING THE PURCHASE

When you have found the land you want to buy and all professional research and advice as well as personal instinct tell you to buy the parcel, you still have to finance the purchase. Obtaining financing to meet your objectives and requirements should be a contingency in a purchase contract.

Ideally, no buyer wants to pay cash for a land purchase, but a seller prefers to receive only cash for the purchase. Invariably, a financial partner or lender is required to make the acquisition and purchase of land a reality.

Speculators, brokers, agents, and land users almost always will look to the seller as their financial partner. Whether or not the seller is an equity participant in the resale or the development of his land, the smart buyer usually wants the seller to finance the purchase.

If this arrangement is not possible with the seller, or if it is advantageous to achieve a lower purchase price, then a solution must be found to finance the purchase.

The financial partner or financier in a land purchase can be any of a multitude of entities from a high income-earning individual to one of the more stoic, prevalent financial institutions.

In fact during the real estate industry's recession of the mid 1970s, savings and loan associations, mutual savings banks, service companies of thrift institutions, commercial banks, and real estate investment trusts all became large landholders. This was not by choice, but because they acquired title to the land by foreclosing on loans made to builders and developers who had offered land as collateral.

If the seller is a financial institution or a large corporation that has banked or otherwise acquired title to land, it is now in a position to provide excellent financing terms or to participate in the profit of reselling or developing the property as a financial venture partner.

SELECTING THE FINANCIAL PARTNER

"If you cannot make a financial partner out of the original landowner," says Nathan Miller of Building and Land Technology Corporation, Ft. Lee, N.J., "then you may want to bring in a professional land speculator. This is his business. All he wants to do is make a profit and do nothing to the land."

According to both Richard L. Weiss and Nathan Miller, the most likely financial partner is a personal acquaintance. "You meet these individuals at country clubs, through business contacts and referrals, attorneys and accountants," Weiss states.

"Consult with the real estate departments of banks, with stockbrokers, insurance companies, and pension funds," Miller recommends. "You'll most likely find a possible land investor among family, friends, the grocer, or even the butcher. They are all possible land investors."

Because it is a lengthy process from the point of initial contractual benefits to the point of the actual development of the land, Weiss believes the financing method should be a joint venture. "The time span requires relaxed capital, and relaxed capital generally is joint-venture capital," Weiss feels. "I believe this will take place with savings and loans, commercial banks, pension funds, and major corporations."

Bruce Nott feels there should be different types of lenders in residential, commercial, industrial, and institutional land purchases:

If you have been in business for a while and have credibility, you probably have a stable of lenders with whom you have done business in the past and who are readily identifiable as to their likes and dislikes. The most likely candidates for residential projects are savings and loans and commercial banks, and for commercial projects, the insurance companies and pension trusts controlled by banks. Of course, there are a large number of high-income earners who want to get in a position where they buy the land and provide the front money and they are in a position to come in at an early point of development, instead of coming on the scene after it is a finished project.

FINANCING BY SUBORDINATION

Simply stated, a partner in a joint land venture should not expect to receive payment on land he has subordinated until it is developed and sold or resold to another party. But William Baker, President of the Florida Land Company, points out that there is a great difference between how the subordination venture is made and whether the land is placed in the venture at cost with no profit or with profit already added to the cost.

"When an owner puts in land at cost, then the two venture partners share in the eventual profit," says Baker. "Another way of subordination is to place the land in the venture with the profit already imputed. During down cycles some owners may put land in at cost or even at less than cost in certain circumstances. However, in a boom period when there is a high demand for land the venture landowner will lock in a profit on his land. It all just depends on the current market conditions."

"When an owner subordinates his land and there is little, if any, underlying debt on the land," according to Irwin Adler, "then he is your partner in every sense of the word; not an operating partner, but a financial partner."

LOOK TO THE OWNER

Martin S. Berger believes that the land seller is the source of the best and lowest cost of financing available to a land speculator or developer:

It has been axiomatic to professionals in the land business that the best potential banker is the farmer or estate owner with whom you are negotiating to acquire a piece of land. As an example, we purchased a parcel of land from a very prominent nursery. The seller had a tremendous land holding with beautiful nursery stock. We structured a five-year program, giving him a period of time in which to take out his nursery stock before we ever started using it. This enabled him to continue deriving income from the property during our period of acquisition.

You also can look to the seller to provide better terms than you might be able to get from conventional lending sources. As a rule of thumb, we look to the seller who already has figured in his profit in the selling price of the land to finance it for us at $2\frac{1}{2}$–3% below the prime rate, with our making a down payment and signing a purchase-money mortgage. If we are unsuccessful in accomplishing this, we can assume a conventional institutional lender will charge us $2\frac{1}{2}$–3% above the prime rate. In other words if the prime rate is $8\frac{1}{2}$%, we would look to buy purchase-money mortgages from the seller at about 6% interest. From an institutional source this would be 11-12%. It all depends again on market conditions.

Berger also believes that it is going to be difficult to encourage institutional partners to provide funds for land financing or venture land acquisitions during the late 1970s.

LANDOWNER OPTIONS

Louis E. Fischer believes that the landowner has two primary considerations:

Either he is interested and willing to become a joint-venture, real estate partner and is in the business of taking his earnings and share of profit, regardless of how long a term that development might take, or he is a landholder who is not in the real estate business and who does not want to get into it but who would prefer to take a capital-gains treatment on the sale of the property. A landowner also can be in the real estate business but be paying ordinary income on the earnings from the sale of property.

The most simple joint venture is when the landholder puts his land in at his actual cost—purchase price *plus* the carrying cost of interest and taxes—and ventures with a professional developer. The developer, who has a track record of performance and who can provide the planning, development, marketing, and ultimate completion of a community, puts all of his inside and outside services in at cost, without any markup. The two venturers jointly arrange financing for the development costs through conventional institutional sources. The profit then is divided 50-50 as it is received, whether it takes 5 years or 25 years. This is a very clean and simple way of doing business.

The other way is when the landowner does not want to be in the real estate business and subordinates his interest in the land to the venture at market value. Market value can be determined by an independent appraisal that is acceptable to both sides. As a developer we then would apply an interest factor and profit to all planning, development, and construction work, as well as a carrying cost for the amount of cash we would have invested. The venture-partner landowner would get paid his asking price for the land, as it is developed and sold, plus his carrying costs of the land in the venture. The partners then are committed to a fixed amount of dollars for the land.

Venture partners are going to be vitally important to builders of all types of real estate in the future. Most companies are terribly sensitive about carrying large inventories of land. Fewer people will be saying "When this recession turns around, we're really going to be in super shape because of all of our inventory." Many companies during the down cycles of the early 1970s were looking only to survive, forcing the redirection of interest toward some form of joint venture or land banking with a financial partner who has the capability and resources to carry the land through down cycles. Builders no longer can continue to expand on a national basis and carry the amount of land inventory they used to believe they could.

UTILIZING CONVENTIONAL LENDING SOURCES

Both Carl A. Rudnick and Ralph Shirley recommend obtaining funds from conventional lending sources to finance land purchases.

"My best possibilities are those I've done business with before, such as savings and loans, commercial banks, or insurance companies," Rudnick states. "It also depends on what the tone of the market is as to the type of financial institution you will want to approach."

Shirley argues that the greatest problem in the industry is the inability of many lending institutions to really understand second lien positions:

For example, I bought a 57-acre parcel of land for $400,000 that I believed was worth $570,000. It cost $165,000 down, and the money was borrowed at a commercial bank, with a financial partner coendorsing the note. There was an existing $215,000 first lien note from the people who had originally purchased the property and who in this case were the sellers. They were personally liable for the $215,000 at 7% interest. My partner and I did not assume the liability for the first lien, but we were obligated to the bank for the $165,000.

The land was acquired at $6500 an acre. I felt it was worth $10,000 an acre when it was tied up, and $12,000 an acre by the time escrow was closed. Within two years we turned down an offer of $15,000 an acre, and later the land was appraised for $17,500 an acre. The carrying costs have been running about $17,000 a year for interest and taxes.

In the third year, my partner decided to get out of the venture, and I needed to refinance the second lien. The total of the two mortgages amounted to $380,000, but the land then was appraised at more than $1 million.

Because many lenders want only a first lien position, I had more than a dozen institutions offer to lend me $600,000 because of the appraisal value, which would have allowed us to walk away with $220,000 cash in hand. The first lien was payable at interest only for two more years and with principal and interest at 7% for ten more years. I was seeking refinancing of the second mortgage so I would be personally liable only for the $165,000 and would have a carry on a total of $380,000, not $600,000. I finally found a good banker who understood land and the real estate business, and he took a secondary position.

The lenders who must understand the business are those who were willingly naive enough to lend me $600,000, to insist that the first lien be paid off as well as the second so there would be a new first lien, and to let me pocket $220,000 cash. In a real down market, those lenders were willing to risk losing $600,000 on the property in the event I would have defaulted. The banker who took the secondary position made a good deal on a loan of $380,000 for property appraised in excess of $1 million.

When bankers say "come borrow money and buy land," then buy all you can buy in a hurry *with their money,* but buy only what you think you can sell."

OTHER FINANCIAL PARTNERS

Ideally, Shirley believes the best financial partners are large corporations, established companies, and reputable individuals, although the purchase may actually be financed by a conventional source. "The financial partner cosigns the note with you and puts up the necessary cash in expectation of a 50% return on the profit of the sale," Shirley reasons.

Some developers and builders choose high-income earners as financial partners to acquire and hold land for capital-gains purposes, signing an agreement that the land is to be purchased in a certain period of time for a specified amount of money. Syndicates and mutual land clubs are other sources of entities that can hold and inventory land for future development, obtaining some tax benefit as well as an anticipated appreciation on investment.

According to Nathan Miller:

A soft dollar to an investor really is half deductible as an expense. It takes the form of interest on mortgages or perhaps real estate taxes compared to hard dollars, which are the equity that goes into the deal itself. Setting up the deal for an investor-partner can be done in such a way that the land purchase may be made with a ten-year payout, without any amortization during the first five years and with amortization of principal and interest during the next five years, giving the investor a five-year write-off.

It also can be structured where there is a higher interest rate at the very outset that decreases each year, starting perhaps at 12% the first year, 11% the second, 10% the third, 9% the fourth, and so on. The deal can be tailored around the investor's needs, particularly when buying from the owner of the land.

Miller believes it is preferable for a real estate developer or builder to find someone else to warehouse the land:

Let's assume you paid $200,000 for a parcel of land ten years ago and sold it for $400,000. Did you really make $200,000 on the sale? Even if you were a sharp buyer, a sharp investor, and used leverage?

On the $200,000 purchase price you probably put down 20%, or $40,000. The seller took back a 7% note with a $100,000 balloon payment due in 1975, ten years later. This would be a fairly common arrangement. In addition to the $200,000 purchase price, over the years the investor would have paid some $46,000 in interest on the note and $40,000 in real estate taxes, after taking a 50% tax deduction against personal income taxes.

When the land was sold for $400,000, a 10% commission on raw land sales would mean $40,000 to the real estate broker. Now the investment isn't $200,000, but $326,000, adding the cost of interest, taxes, and brokerage commission.

However, the investor is still $73,000 ahead. But when computing profit you still have to deduct a capital-gains tax of 30–35%, and on a supposed profit of $150,000, the Internal Revenue Service takes $48,000, bringing the net ten-year investment profit down to $25,450.

Had the same investor deposited the $40,000 down payment in a savings account, ten years later it would be worth $12,500 after taxes. I have to question whether the extra $13,000 was worth the risk and patience. Might not tax free municipals at 5–6% have been a better bet? Even assuming you paid the $200,000 in cash and didn't have to carry any expense of the note, you still would have been better off putting cash in municipals.

Miller cites another company project:

As land packagers we assembled a tract of 60 acres and had to put up $50,000 on contract. The property was zoned for half-acre lots. We paid $6500 an acre. While the property was zoned for half-acre lots, it was not economically buildable or feasible as a single-family development.

Unfortunately, we could not negotiate a contract with contingencies, nor could we negotiate a closing date later than one year. We didn't know whether or not we could achieve rezoning in one year. The terms were pretty stiff. Our feasibility studies showed a market for townhouses, and we felt there was a 50-50 possibility that the local municipal government would agree. However, we couldn't risk in any way the exposure of putting up the cash within a year if we hadn't accomplished our purpose.

We decided to look for an investor-partner, and actually found two. The three of us formed a joint venture with the partners providing the funding for the processing and titles as necessary. The key was that if we did not achieve the results even on half-acre zoning, with inflation and because of the important location of the property the investors would come out well. However, within the year we did successfully rezone the property at ten units to the acre. We had invested $50,000 in planning and engineering. The project was sold to a major national builder, who paid $20,000 an acre, or a profit of $13,500 an acre less costs for the project. Furthermore, we never took title to the land. The builder took title directly from the owner. By using a middleman, we were able to take the risk out of the deal for our company, settle for less profit, but come out winners in the end.

VENTURE GUIDELINES

Miller suggests that if you are going to become involved in a holding operation with a monied partner, the venture must be fully financed at the outset to hold the land. "Don't set up an entity where the financial partners do not have enough money to take title, or have option money to hold the property until you may have to take title. Make sure there is sufficient funding to carry through to the ultimate objective.

"A builder-user should not set up a land venture unless the property has a 50-50 chance of obtaining approval within three years. Be selective in the choice of land, the location, the access to utilities, transportation, and the marketing potential. Also be sure to check out the soil conditions and the title."

Miller believes that to be a successful joint venture the property must be sold mutually within a five-year period for twice the original purchase price of the raw land.

CHAPTER VIII

LAND BANKING

Land banking is the long-term control of a large parcel of land, held in a natural or an interim state, by an investor who speculates that the land can be sold or developed at a profit.

From the post World War II real estate boom until the early 1970s, land banking presented the greatest profit opportunities for the speculator, as well as for the builder and developer who must be assured of a readily available supply of raw land.

The real estate industry, and especially the important segment of it related to residential housing, has always been cyclical. Real estate depends on a number of uncontrollable and seldom anticipated factors, most particularly the availability of and the cost of money, and government regulation.

The largest single users of land are residential developers and builders. These companies consider land banking an ideal hedge against inflation and a means of protection against the spiraling costs of labor and materials, where the increased value of the land would assure a profitable development or project.

The housing industry has had good and bad years. During the decade of the 1950s and 1960s, land was a viable investment that almost always continued to increase in value.

From 1950–1959, the industry built 14.71 million new housing units, but fell nearly 300,000 units short of this figure from 1960–1969 when it produced only 14.43 million units. The housing industry appeared to be well on its way to an era of spectacular growth with the passage of the omnibus Housing Act of 1968. For once the nation's housing goals were clearly defined and established by Congress, which projected a ten-year need of 26 million new and rehabilitated units in the 1970s—an amount almost equal to the total number of housing units the industry had produced the last 20 years.

Special government committees, including The President's Committee on Urban Housing (Kaiser Committee), The National Commission on Civil Disorders (Kerner Commission), and The National Commission on Urban Problems (Douglas Commission), all emphasized the tremendous need for new housing throughout America.

The Housing Act of 1968 provided housing programs for almost every socioeconomic group, ranging from subsidized rental and subsidized home-ownership programs to utopic new towns.

Almost concurrent with the enactment of this milestone legislation, a new type of residential builder and developer emerged, who was quickly defined as the "professional housing producer." This new type of builder introduced innovative concepts in management, marketing, and financing to the housing industry. Where the residential housing industry had long been a fragmented and a highly localized business, companies began to expand and to operate on a nationwide basis.

With definite goals outlined by Congress and with administrative encouragement given to the private sector to achieve housing objectives, many companies in the industry developed an insatiable appetite for land almost overnight. Land was needed for expansion into new markets and for product diversification. And land had to be ready when it was needed. Everyone believed that land prices would soon be prohibitive, even if a seller could be found.

During this same period, many professional housing producers offered their company stock for sale to the public. These new housing stocks were immediately categorized by Wall Street as glamour stocks. Wall Street also pressured the companies for compounded growth rates never before achieved in the industry. The financial community insisted on five-year projections and wanted to know when, where, and how the growth would materialize into profits and earnings. Instead of land banking on a highly local or regional basis, companies began land banking on a national basis.

One exception to this widely promulgated rule of the necessity to land bank was Eli Broad, whose corporate philosophy at Kaufman and Broad, Inc., in Los Angeles was to treat land as a raw-material commodity. Land banking requires tremendous outlays of capital, and Broad felt this capital could be better used elsewhere. Land was acquired when and where it was needed, just as Kaufman and Broad, Inc., acquired lumber, roofing, appliances, and other components it required for construction.

THE CRASH OF THE 1970s

By 1970 taxes and interest had increased astronomically to the point where, for the first time in 25 years, the cost of carrying land exceeded its appreciation value. From 1965–1974 interest rates nearly doubled. Property tax assessors began to place more realistic market values on buildable land; combined with spiraling property tax rates, this factor increased greatly.

The advent of environmentalists and ecologists during the early 1970s compounded the problem of land banking. Local governments began to require various economic and environmental impact reports and other studies, and additional layers of bureaucratic approval lengthened the development process to what some people regarded as an eternity.

Eli Broad's outspoken views, so diametrically opposed to the general rule of the industry, proved correct when the industry began to crash in late 1973 after three successive years of more than two million new housing starts.

Many large, national builders soon discovered that land was no longer an asset; it was a liability. Instead of a 5-year inventory, companies had sufficient land for 10, 15, or even more years. Richard L. Weiss states:

There wasn't a single major builder or developer that would not have sold you land for less than his book value in 1974 and 1975. Three or four years before, the same company had paid a premium for that land.

Land today is not appreciating at a rate rapid enough to break even. For example, when the prime rate jumped to as high as 12%, the total carrying costs, including taxes, interest, and the premium points a developer pays over prime, was 20% or more. This means if a company has $100 million of land inventory, it has to make $20 million a year after taxes just to break even.

The practice of stockpiling land or even holding sufficient land for one's needs is a very risky business. It not only inhibits profitability and cash flow, but the period of time necessary to accomplish zoning and political approvals. Unless and until the time comes that the carrying cost of land can be related to in terms of the accumulation of cárrying costs and time required to bring land to development, and these combined costs can be absorbed into the development so there still is a profit at the end, then land banking for a builder or developer will not be a favorable enterprise for some time to come.

Ronald Foell of the Standard-Pacific Corporation, Costa Mesa, California, believes that most operative builders cannot afford to do their own land banking anymore. "The cost of carrying land these days is generally more than the appreciation of the land. Also, the cash flows involved in land banking are beyond the scope of most building companies.

"If you buy a big piece of land out in the country with the idea of holding it for ultimate development, there are so many problems these days relative to utility extensions, incorporations, schools, transportation, and the environment that it may never come to pass during the time you allocated for the development process," says Foell. "I don't believe you can afford to land bank unless the land has an interim use that will pay for the carrying costs."

Paul T. Pohly believes a developer should not inventory land unless he is capable of reselling it. "If I go into raw ground, I have to take all of my costs, and the risk is a multiple factor of 3. I add all of my carrying costs and then multiply by 3, and that is the retail price I must receive," he says. "However, land banking is probably the most profitable investment today for the person who has excess cash. A corporation that has excess cash should be in land, and land banking will be profitable if it is judiciously bought."

Major publicly held corporations that decided to diversify by acquiring or starting a real estate operation in 1974 also found they held staggeringly large parcels of land that were virtually unmanageable.

Cash flow is most critical in real estate management, and land banking demands financial strength. Lending institutions foreclosed on the land assets of builders and developers who did not have the financial staying power to weather the crush of the 1973–1974 recession. Consequently, lending institutions have become large landowners, and many may even profit handsomely from their unchosen acquisitions.

LAND BANKING: A NEW INDUSTRY

Because of the tremendous amounts of cash and financial strength needed to acquire land and to pay the interest and taxes required to hold land for long periods of time, the real estate industry will witness the development of a new concept in land banking in the future.

Residential builders will probably heed the advice of Eli Broad, originally espoused in the mid-1960s, to only buy land for a specific purpose. The professional land banker will emerge and grow to become a new industry within the industry. The land banker will be a financially oriented investor with tremendous amounts of capital, projected cash flow, and a willingness and an ability to wait a number of years for his return on investment.

Michael I. Keston, President of The Larwin Group, Inc., Encino, California, believes that institutions such as oil companies, large corporations unrelated to real estate, insurance companies, and pension funds will be the land bankers of tomorrow. "The builder will pay the top price for land, buying it as a packaged commodity when he needs it."

Samuel Primack, partner of The Perl-Mack Companies in Denver, predicts that financial service institutions will become major land bankers who acquire land and lease it for development. "They will lease the land based on actuarial studies to amortize their returns. They will put in the community amenities, which is the only viable way a sizable new community project will be able to be developed.

"The builder will put in the product, working in the same manner as he would in buying a finished lot, ready to go," says Primack. "The individual homeowner will be responsible for the ad valorem taxes. This is one way housing costs can be reduced. The cost of a $7000 or more finished lot will be spread over a period of 50 years or more. We will be applying a lease concept that has proved successful for years for commercial and other properties in central urban areas."

William Nolan of Philadelphia envisions a land bank investor as a third entity in what he believes will become a new real estate field. "The land banker will acquire or control the land and work with a developer who has the expertise to do a master plan concept. The developer also will help market the land to the builder, who will provide the shelter.

"The land banker, in addition to having the financial staying power, must have a level of political sophistication to realistically understand what can be accomplished with the land," says Nolan.

Nolan sees a typical land-bank concept of the future as, for example, five holdings of 2000 acres in five different geographic locations, rather than one large 10,000-acre holding. "If you get a turnaround in a local administration or new government, the entire 10,000 acres could be in trouble," he says. "I would rather take my chances of having one in trouble with four that are still working. The land banker will be the person taking the risk, but he will be compensated and rewarded accordingly."

According to Louis E. Fischer, companies involved in the development and sale of residential land will no longer acquire thousands of acres for long-term use. "When land was purchased 20 years ago for anywhere from $40 to $100 an acre, companies could calculate the interest expense and taxes and the financial affect of carrying land over a 20-year period." he says. "With the uncertainties of the regulatory agencies and the directions they might take in the years ahead, I don't believe any company can realistically afford to buy and carry large amounts of land, even at $2000 an acre."

Some companies that were not originally oriented to real estate have become so in recent years, including large landowners such as railroads, oil and timber companies, and public utilities. In addition to lending institutions and financial-service companies, including insurance companies, these large landholders may emerge as the land bankers of tomorrow, because they will have cash assets, cash flow, and financial staying power.

Much of the land in ITT's Palm Coast development was acquired and used for many years by another ITT division that was not involved in real estate. Penn Central and Southern Pacific are two examples of railroads that have become involved in various types of real estate developments; public utilities with land holdings include the Florida Land Company, a subsidiary of the Florida Gas Company, and Fredericks Development, a subsidiary of Pacific Lighting.

SHORT-TERM, SPOT-PARCEL LAND BANKING

A new concept that is emerging in land banking is the purchase of selected parcels of land to be held for shorter terms. The real estate division of a major, publicly held oil company utilizes the cash of its parent organization to profit in land. The company purchases already zoned parcels of land, generally not in excess of 100 acres, for cash and sells them, usually for cash, within two to five years.

As an example, one company's researchers determined that a new four-lane highway was to be built in a particular city and that a major intersection would be created at some point in time. A local speculator who owned 100 acres had held the land for some time and was interested in selling. The company agreed to purchase the site if the seller would have a piece of the land zoned for a gasoline station and the balance of the acreage zoned for commercial and multifamily residences. The company paid the seller $10,000 cash per acre and built the gasoline station. Two years later the road was completed, traffic had increased, and the company sold 40 acres of the land for apartment development. The company has subsequently sold sites for franchised fast-food service operations and for a convenience or strip shopping center. Most sales transactions were in cash, as was the original purchase of the land.

The company does not normally work with local real estate brokers, but it does work closely with the premiere real estate attorney and the real estate lender in the community.

INDIVIDUAL INVESTMENT OPPORTUNITIES

Opportunities exist for high income-earning individuals to buy and carry land for developers and builders. Real estate companies that wish to have buildable land available when it is needed can provide capital-gains opportunities for high income-earning individuals or the partnerships they form. This formula is not commonly used in the industry, it is by no means a new concept. These individuals may be U.S. citizens who are seeking only capital gains and who are willing to pay tax on the appreciation. In addition off-shore money is available from foreign investors who are not seeking tax shelter and who, as nonresidents, have no opportunity to do so. The Canadian government's tax on land investment and transactions has almost forced Canadians to place their money in U.S. land investments in recent years, virtually acting as a financial partner for a real estate building and development company. Richard L. Weiss explains:

The high income-earning individual can buy and carry the property and the developer can have an option to purchase it back at a fixed price. This will enable the high income earner to have the incremental difference between his cost, the carrying cost, and a profit at the end. It can be either an absolute commitment to buy out the individual, or it can be a first refusal, so the investor can sell the land to someone else; the developer has the right of first refusal to purchase the land.

These individuals are met at country clubs, through contacts, referral, parties, mutual attorneys, and accountants. Acquaintanceship. Each way that one goes is smart if it fits the particular circumstances of the project at hand. And the next week, the same developer and same monied individual might do something differently or follow some other alternative. There is no absolute pattern.

The U.S. Home Corporation in Clearwater, Florida, is one publicly held building firm that has dealt successfully with high income-earning Canadian professionals. Charles Rutenberg, U.S. Home's Chairman, states:

When we see a parcel of land we know we want and plan to develop, we will contact high income-earning individuals with whom we have worked in the past.

Many are Canadian professionals or businessmen. They will acquire the land based on our recommendations. We will buy the land from the investor group when we plan.to build on it, providing the investors with an appreciation on their investment. If necessary, we will assist on obtaining the desired zoning and environmental approvals. This enables us to control land without laying out cash or the cost of the land carry.

It also helps keep our balance sheets clean, because we have no obligation whatsoever to buy the land from the investor group at any time. They must assume the risk that we will ever purchase the land, but based on our past performance in working with such groups, there is a mutual trust. The investor can anticipate a certain percentage gain on his investment, and we have land when we want it, paying no more than we would in the open market and sometimes even less than if we had bought it as ready-to-build land. Both parties benefit.

Individual land bankers will become almost as common in future years as the new breed of institutional land banking organizations. The institution will decide what land to purchase and when, and the individual will rely on the advice and direction of his builder-"partner," who eventually will be the purchaser and the end user.

INTERIM-USE LAND BANKING

Creating uses for land to derive income while it is being banked is not a new concept either. With the ever-increasing cost of carrying land, speculators and land bankers have become much more creative in making the greatest profits from any land they hold or control.

The important consideration is to find a use for the land that will produce sufficient revenue to offset the costs of interest and taxes and that will amortize any improvements made on the land to derive this income.

Major builders and developers often overlook the possibility of interim-use land banking, because within large organizations it would necessitate additional staff overhead that would not be compensated by the additional revenue. Individual speculators, partnerships, syndicates, and smaller, entrepreneurial companies have taken advantage of various interim-use, income-producing opportunities.

"The problem with most builders and developers over the years has been that if an attractive piece of land comes their way and they can get the financing, they grab it without any consideration of the downside risk," Martin S. Berger states. In one business-industrial park developed by the Robert Martin Corporation, Berger cited how land recycling was planned. "We have built warehouses and provided excess parking areas on the theory that ten years later we can convert some of the warehouses to office structures at tremendous increments in rent, but it is essential that we have the parking space now for the office use. In a warehouse zone you normally provide one parking space for each 1000 square feet of building, but in an office area you need three parking spaces for each 1000 square feet of space. When we're ready for the conversion, we will have the necessary parking and very little additional cost for improvements in relation to the increased per-square-foot rental of the buildings."

David Riese cites rental apartments as one means of interim land use that gives the owners certain tax advantages. "An apartment project does have a 20- or 30-year life before it becomes obsolete and no longer provides a tax or income return for the investor," he says. "In one major metropolitan area one investor has acquired between 7000 and 8000 apartment units in the inner city, where there has been significant growth. He bought them because of the eventual use for the land, and at the same time had the income from the rental units offsetting the expense of the purchase and carry."

Bruce E. Nott believes that mobile-home parks provide an excellent opportunity for interim land use. He has acquired land projects with growth opportunities that eventually become expensive, high-density residential or commercial property. "There are examples by the dozens of properties that were developed as mobile-home parks in the 1950s and even in the early 1960s in California, Arizona, and Florida," says Nott.

"In one case in Florida land was purchased in 1951 for $1500 an acre and built as a 200-space mobile-home park. In 1972 that same site sold for $12 a square foot, or for more than $500,000 an acre for the site of a high-rise condominium. The return on that initial investment was infinity, because the net income from the mobile-home project was between $180,000 and $200,000 a year," he said.

William E. Becker also believes mobile-home parks offer an excellent opportunity for interim land use, especially if the land will not be developed for seven years. "Why seven years?" questions Becker. "Because with a mobile home I can get good financing for seven years, and depending on the market, all the improvements such as streets, utilities, and others can be amortized. Where most companies go wrong with land is that they take the land into inventory before they need it or can effectively utilize it during the interim period.

Bruce E. Nott also cites farming as a valuable interim land use:

I know strawberry farmers who have made as high as $8000–$10,000 an acre in one year. I know there are examples that go the other way, but if you are an extremely confident farmer you can go into areas today where farming is going on land priced at $40,000 an acre and even $100,000 an acre. The farmer is making a good return and is paying his taxes.

I will entertain land banking if I can buy land at a good price today and can use it, but I will not consider bringing outside money into land to hold it while I try to decide what to do with it. If I can't get the original owner to hold at what I consider to be favorable rates—below bank rates—then I'm not interested in speculating either with passive money that is outside of my business or with my company's money. Land banking, by the standards judged in 1965, and land banking today have no comparison. It is a dangerous business, and you must know what you are doing and how to profit until the land is ready for sale or development.

Architect Robert Martin Engelbrecht is also a strong believer in utilizing land for agricultural purposes while it is being land banked for a future use. "One mutual land club our firm counseled immediately converted the raw land to a tree farm, not only to cover the carrying costs but for profit motivation as well.

"Agriculture is an enormous area of investment right now, where people are investing in land in which they have a tenant farmer or a corporation to manage the farming operations. If you accumulate land in a location where it can be used for agriculture and also can be cropped in with wood, it carries itself," according to Engelbrecht.

Residents of Arizona, California, and Florida have long seen citrus crops disappear into real estate developments of one kind or another. Many syndicates in the mid-1960s sold citrus farming as a tax-sheltered investment to carry the land until it could be sold for an appreciable capital gain.

Engelbrecht is a strong believer in making raw land pay for itself during land-banking periods. "If it cannot be used for agricultural purposes, then consider cattle or horse breeding or other types of ranching." Engelbrecht points out that only creativity is needed to come up with the right idea. As examples he cites large acreage that can be used seasonally for entertainment or recreational purposes, including fairs, open-air concerts, motorcycle or bicycle motocrosses, recreational-vehicle rental space, and even hang-glider sporting events.

Harry Kwartler suggests interim land uses that amortize the improvements and handle the carrying costs of short-term land banking. "A golf driving range leaves the land in its relatively natural state, generally on a major highway or road that is zoned commercially and in an area that has not been built up to its peak. When the area around it builds up, then change the use of the property.

"A drive-in theater will be a viable investment in itself, if you can get a major chain to lease it from you," he advises. "Tennis has become extremely popular, and the cost of outdoor tennis courts can be amortized during the holding period." Kwartler also suggests considering a used-car, mobile-home, or recreational-vehicle lot during an interim-use period for land that could eventually become a regional or a neighborhood shopping center.

For inner-city land parking lots provide an opportunity to land bank commercial property. The cost of demolishing the existing structure normally does not result in an expense, but in many cases contracting with a demolition firm can produce a profit. The vacant space can then be leased for a number of years to pay the carrying costs. With the technology of portable parking structures, a five-year period would probably produce a profit without consideration of the increased value of the land during the holding time.

Kwartler believes that improvements can be made on certain inner-city land and that the value of the land must be related to the type of improvement to be placed on the site as a holding device. "For example, in New York City on a high-rise office site where the land value can be $50 a foot, it is not uncommon for a large urban developer to put a one-story building on it to cover the tax payments," he says. "In some areas you can build a 10,000-square-foot, one-story building for $20 a square foot. But it would not be out of line to spend $300,000 or even $400,000 on a piece of land valued at $5 million. The cost has to relate to some percentage of the value of the land."

Interim land uses for land investment bankers could include:

- Warehouses
- Rental apartments
- Agriculture and farming
- Ranching and grazing
- Mobile-home parks
- Parking lots
- One-story buildings in inner cities
- Golf driving ranges
- Indoor or outdoor tennis or paddle-tennis courts
- Used-car, recreational-vehicle, or mobile-home lots
- Drive-in theaters
- Childrens' day camps
- Rock concerts
- Open-air theater productions
- Motorcycle or bicycle motocrosses
- Recreational-vehicle campgrounds

- Fairs
- Sporting events
- Par-3 golf courses
- Miniature golf courses
- Coin-operated amusement centers
- Car washes
- Franchised fast-foodservice outlets
- Swim-tennis clubs
- Go-cart racing courses
- Swap meets

Interim land uses should also be considered whenever a real estate developer or builder faces a setback in zoning or an unforeseen delay that turns months of development into years. A number of opportunities exist to put land to the use for which it may be zoned, without seeking various bureaucratic approvals, to produce income to reduce the loss carry during the approval period.

Real estate developers should also consider using vacant land to improve public service during land-banking or holding periods. Problems should not be viewed as problems, but as opportunities. In many residential areas vacant land can be used for pocket vegetable or flower gardens. This not only builds community spirit and further enhances the aesthetic appearance of the neighborhood, but is is also a means of winning that very important government approval.

Residential builders also continue to overlook opportunities in adjacent and contiguous land parcels that are months or even years away from development and that are accessible to tracts currently being developed. These parcels can also serve as community pocket farms to openly represent the developer's social conscience. Such planning represents little, if any, additional cost. It is not only good business; it is also good common sense.

CHAPTER IX

BUYING LAND AS
A PACKAGED COMMODITY

The concept of buying land that is ready to use is the antithesis of land banking. Ready-to-use, buildable land is free from any legal encumbrances that would prevent development and is zoned for the intended improvement. All necessary approvals and permits are in order, and construction can begin without delay.

The land can be a single lot for a commercial office building or an apartment, a larger parcel to accommodate a series of buildings, such as a shopping center or an industrial park, a series of lots in a small or medium-sized tract for residential housing, or lots in a subdivision that is part of a larger, planned community development or a new town.

Few residential community builders exclusively practice one land-acquisition concept. A company's management philosophy may be contrary to land banking, but if a unique opportunity arises the company may acquire land with a specific use in mind, although construction may not be planned for two, three, or even four more years.

Kaufman and Broad, Inc., is a leading proponent of buying land as a packaged commodity. "We want raw land in a state of usability when we are ready to start construction," Eli Broad explains. Naturally, a higher price is paid for land that is zoned and that contains utilities than is paid for raw land, because the risk that the land may never be purchased for its intended use has already been taken by another investor. Someone has also already invested the capital required to acquire or to control the land and has paid the high cost required to carry and inventory the land until it is developed or sold.

The Kaufman and Broad philosophy is to control ready-to-use, buildable land with an available inventory for approximately 18 months in an area where there are active development programs. Short-term inventories can fluctuate according to management objectives. In a down production cycle when housing starts are off, this may be a period of only eight months. Conversely, the cycle could be extended as much as two years in a period of increasing sales when high demand and available money are anticipated.

The number of buildable lots controlled by Kaufman and Broad, regardless of the type of acquisition agreement or method, is based directly on the company's projected number of housing starts in any paricular region, location, or development.

The Standard-Pacific Corporation purchases relatively small parcels of land on which residential construction can begin immediately and attempts to complete its projects within an 18-month period. Ronald Foell, corporate President explains:

> Our philosophy is to purchase land that already has the amenities, where the value can be readily ascertained and subject to a sufficient number of contengencies, so we are not obligated to pay for the land until we are ready to start construction and have all necessary municipal approvals.
>
> When we look for amenities, we not only want utilities within a reasonable distance of the site, with a capacity to handle the proposed number of units to be built, but other necessary ancillary improvements. These include commercial shopping centers, churches, schools, available public transportation, and easy access to major streets and roads.

Richard L. Weiss believes a company must develop an objective as to how much land it plans to control, acquire, and carry, as well as a timetable for land development and completion. "The closer you can come to that objective, the better off your business enterprise will be," Weiss advises.

As an example, he cites the possibility of short-term land control, where current inventory would require no longer than three years to begin the construction process and no longer than five years to complete it.

"Businessmen fail to understand that land is not fungible," Weiss says. "One piece of land is unique and different from any other piece of land. You can't always rush out and buy land to immediately fill your particular needs, like a machine shop would need to buy steel for an order not previously anticipated. In the case of the machine shop it might have to pay a premium to get a particular type and standard of steel, but it can be bought. You might not be able to get land at the time you need it, at the right place, and with the right terms and conditions."

LAND PACKAGES

Land-packaging companies offer a new dimension to land brokerage by providing residential builders with land when they are ready to build on it or when they have a specific timetable for construction. The land packager helps to plan the most profitable land use and performs rezoning work when necessary. The builder takes title to the land when he needs it.

A leading land-packaging company is the Building and Land Technology Corporation in Paramus, N.J. The company performs land-acquisition and brokerage functions, but its larger service is helping to create land-use plans that will be approved by local communities.

"Builders can fall flat on their face in buying land today, even if they are experts in dickering with farmers," says Nathan J. Miller, chairman of Building and Land Technology. "Skill in finding acreage and negotiating with the owners remains necessary. But more important today is the expertise in getting the land processed through government agencies and public bodies so it can be used for building.

"Planning today requires a knowledge of the community and its problems first. If you cannot come up with a package that is advantageous to the community, the likelihood of success for the optimum use of land is slim," Miller explains.

Most large-volume residential builders who acquire land only when they are ready to build can place more management emphasis on construction, quality control, marketing, and financing by relying on a land packager or a land technologist.

According to Miller, land technology is not land banking, land speculation, or land development, and it does not involve retail lot sales. "Primarily it means control of the acquisition of raw land, the determination of optimal use and processing of that land through all the zoning, planning, and design techniques that may be necessary to obtain all government approvals, so that building permits will be granted," he says.

Miller points out that during the 1950s and 1960s the cost per unit for processing land was approximately $25, excluding bonding, surveying, and final calculated maps. "Now that figure is more like $150 per housing unit, not counting executive time and talent. Marketing costs might run $300 per unit, plus up-front risk," Miller adds.

Builders who work with land packagers can ensure that land is controlled, processed, and available for construction without becoming involved in large land inventories or bearing the cost of carrying such acreage or the cost of management overhead required to handle all process and approval functions.

Another concept that may become more common is a triumvirate approach in which the builder, the land packager, and the investor or investor group work in concert. Instead of carrying raw land themselves, builders work with packagers to syndicate land to investors, with a guarantee that the builder can use the land for future development. In the meantime needed capital is not tied up in purchasing or holding the land parcels.

Being able to acquire or control valuable property when needed, without holding costs, can contribute to viable long-term development planning. Because the costs of warehousing land are becoming more burdensome each year, holding costs through syndication are relatively minor in relation to the residual gains in value and in this way land can be a profitable investment. If the acreage planned for future use is controlled by a syndicate, the builder can repurchase the land from the investors when it is needed for development or can even include the investors as limited partners in the development enterprise. The land packager works with the investors to schedule and secure land approval, so that the parcel is ready for use based on the builder's operational projections.

THE NEW TOWN OR COMMUNITY APPROACH

The function of the land packager and the land technologist is extended greatly when a land banker or land developer creates a new town or a new planned community.

The social, economic, physical, and governmental aspects of the new town or community must be preplanned. The land use extends far beyond residential housing. Depending on the size of the acreage involved, it will contain a variety of residential projects: commercial shopping centers, free-standing commercial buildings and even office buildings, recreational facilities, schools, churches, parks, and an employment base for industrial, professional, and service job opportunities.

Generally, the entire concept of a new town or community is committed to paper, and a course of developmental action is planned. Land already zoned is then sold to a builder, who improves the raw land based on the community's general plan as to where the residential, commercial, industrial, recreational, and other ancillary projects are to be built.

Although the success and profitability of new towns has been viewed with adversity and skepticism in recent years, many planned new communities have in effect become viable new towns. Perhaps the largest, most diversified, and most successful planned new community in the nation is the 130-square-mile, 83,000-acre Irvine Ranch in California's Orange County. Kenneth W. Agid, Director of Residential Marketing for the Irvine Company:

> At Irvine the builder is only an interim user of the land who never receives title to the properties in our residential communities. We have the right to control and direct the activities that take place on the land during the construction period. The developer pays rent on the land and assumes responsibility for all finance charges, including property taxes and connection charges for improvements such as sewer and water put in by the public agencies.
>
> The builder makes arrangements for his construction financing, but does not have to worry about major front-end costs. As the new residences are completed and sold, the builder then pays off his construction loan and our land cost.
>
> If a builder does not live up to his part of the agreement, by not building a product according to plan, then we have the right to pull our our land from the agreement.

These controls not only benefit the landowner, who wants to ensure the quality of a new community, they are also important to the builder who decides to operate in such an environment. They assure a builder that the master plan is being executed the way it was conceived.

According to Agid, the Irvine Company also provides extensive planning, marketing, and promotional direction for the builders with whom it works. "We can do regional market research and planning, because we have 130 square miles that we are monitoring. We can guide a builder into exactly the program that makes sense, let him know what type of product the consumer wants, and continue to give him information on precisely what the new-home buyer wants in a new house."

A new town or a community can also be planned to prevent an overbuilt situation in which housing supply far exceeds housing demand. "One of the things we now build into our programs is building smaller increments," says Agid. "We may only commit to a builder sufficient land for 50 or 75 units and make no further agreement until we can see the results, the absorption rate, and acceptance in the marketplace."

Continuing market research and control over architectural design and floor plans prevents too much sameness and affords the builder a more custom-unique product. Agid emphasizes the fact that ten different builders operated in an area of 400 acres at Irvine, each with a different set of floor plans, or a total of 45 different plans in the project. "As we moved into the next quadrant of the community, we deleted the products the consumer liked least and further refined and improved the most popular eight or ten plans," Agid explains "We don't want 600 look-alikes in any one area."

The major problem inherent in developing a new community is the tremendous amount of capital that is required in the initial planning and development phases. This investment will not generate a cash return for many years to come. Owners of such large land holdings are also exposed to the harassment and intimidation of no-growth advocates and to the political risk that the "government" of the new residents in the community could always change their master development plan.

There are many advantages for the builder involved in the development of a new community. In addition to eliminating much of the initial cash investment and planning and market support, a builder entering a new market can save one to three years in beginning the construction program and can work in an established community in which values are readily assessed. If the program in the community is successful, the builder has the added advantage of being part of an ongoing success.

TYPES OF NEW COMMUNITIES

In 1974 the New Communities Council of the Urban Land Institute defined the following categories for new towns.

Satellite New Community.   The *Satellite new community* is an adjunct of a larger metropolitan area on which it relies for many of its essential elements. The satellite new community is not self-sufficient; it is not a complete community in the full sense of the word. Its economy and social life are inextricably tied to the larger community, of which it is a somewhat detached but integral element.

Freestanding New Community.   Located in an area distant from any urban center, the *freestanding new community* incorporates all the social and organizational elements necessary to indepenent existence. Its size and economic function depend on the region in which it is located and on the purpose for which it was created.

New-Town-In-Town. The *new-town-in-town* is a large-scale, multiuse development incorporated within the fabric of an existing community. This type of new community is different from other redevelopment efforts in that it represents a conscious effort to create a self-sufficient community with its own identity within the urban environment. An essential feature of the new-town-in-town is that it affords a significant number of its residents the opportunity to both live and work within its boundaries.

"Company" New Community. The *"company" new community* is a residential community developed by a corporation as an adjunct of an industrial operation in an undeveloped area where conventional communities are absent. The specialized nature of the "company" new community distinguishes it from the freestanding new community, which the "company" community resembles in other respects. Towns developed to house workers in the mineral-extracting industry are perhaps most representative of this new type of community.

Growth Center. Where an existing community is used as the nucleus of a new community, it may be described as a *growth center* or an *"add-on-new" community*. The expansion of the original community would have to be great enough to become the dominant element in the resulting new community.

CHAPTER X

THE RISK OF CHANGING
POLITICAL ENVIRONMENTS

Anyone who buys land for investment or development must recognize that even though the land may have an intended use or the potential to be improved in a particular way, every community or state has tools at its disposal to control and direct the development process.

Until 1970 the general public was not fully aware that land use, either good or bad, affects a wide spectrum of environmental, economic, social, and political concerns. Local communities exercised well-established and well-known land-use controls, and even the most traditional controls such as restrictive or discriminatory zoning were not changed or refined until very recently. Many other tools available to a government are new or relatively untried. Some are promising; obvious pitfalls are inherent in others. In many cases the impact and affect when these controls are implemented by a government are essentially irreversible.

FACTORS AFFECTING VALUE

The buyer must be aware of the environmental, economic, social, and political influences that can dramatically affect the value and marketability of land between the time of purchase and the proposed sale or development phase. Important factors present today (and to be with us in the near future) that can affect the potential end use and development of land include energy, municipal services, environmental considerations, and no-growth or slow-growth pressures.

Energy.   No one could really have predicted the impact of the energy crisis on the United States. For once, Americans became aware of the nation's dependency on oil as well as on natural gas. Without electricity, there can be no development, and the shortage of natural gas in many areas has resulted in moratoriums on all types of land development. Local governments that owned municipal utilities that were not assured an adequate supply of natural gas or oil for conversion to electricity or of natural gas for direct consumption simply stopped issuing building permits.

Municipal Services.   Whether or not a local government provides certain essential municipal services determines the value and buildability of a parcel of land. Water must be available. In most instances a connection must be made to existing sewer lines. If the local government wishes to curtail or to control development, it can simply elect not to extend water or sewer facilities or it can limit these connections by specific design.

The right of a town or a city to control its own growth has been challenged in the courts. Later in this chapter cases involving Ramapo, N.Y., Belle Terre, N.Y., and Petaluma, California are discussed. A recent study reported that nearly 20% of all local governments surveyed imposed some type of moratorium on building permits or sewer connections.

A local community must also know what economic impact the proposed development will have on its school system, its public transportation system, and fire, police, and other necessary public services. Many landowners and developers spend years in court before they finally realize that some governmental decisions that seem unconstitutional can be irreversible.

Environmental Considerations.   The requirement of an Environmental Impact Report not only extends the time of development, but also becomes an added expense questioned by some landowners and developers. Other landholders believe there are no established guidelines or qualified professionals to judge the merits and demerits of any EIR, because the accuracy of the report cannot be determined until years after a project has been completed. State and federal government agencies impose a number of environmental controls on land, including the Environmental Protection Agency and the National Flood Insurance Act.

Land developers must answer many environmental questions to the satisfaction of regulatory agencies and public-interest groups. Will development create any ecological problems that will affect air or water purity, vegetation, or wildlife habitat? Will there be sufficient drainage? What are the present and proposed soil and topographical conditions? Can the location be defined as critical for public use?

No-Growth and Slow-Growth Pressures.   Some organizations and even some governments are opposed to any growth or new development in their localities. Every two, three, or four years, a city council or a board of supervisors can change the legal structure and philosophy regarding degree of development. The landowner must consider the interrelationship between the proposed development and community goals, economic forces, tax policies, and land-use controls. Are the arguments of the no-growth, slow-growth philosophy valid or merely a form of harassment?

Some communities have adapted the most extreme form of this philosophy: they want no more growth and consequently no more development in their localities. The no-growth approach is a futile community concept over time. The question that naturally arises is whether the community can deny an owner the right to the reasonable use of his land; such a denial of right could be considered a violation of the Constitution unless the owner is compensated for his loss by the community. When the local decision is to defer growth by temporarily suspending building or development, the courts tend to support the community.

"The fact that a person owns a piece of land no longer ensures that he will have the right to use the land, because of the growing political and environmental pressures of no growth and slow growth," says Sanford R. Goodkin of the Sanford R. Goodkin Research Corporation, Del Mar, California. "Literally each time a planning commission or city council meets in America, costs are added to develop a parcel of land or to improve the land with new construction. The risk is no longer in terms of whether or not you have a marketplace for a piece of land, but whether or not the local municipality will allow any use of the land."

All aspects of land research and analysis can indicate a buy situation, but a thorough, qualitative analysis may not reveal some of the problems that could confront a land developer in even the first 12 months of ownership.

Some land, by virtue of its location or proposed use, may be particularly vulnerable to political delays and moratoriums. In such cases deciding whether or not the land can even be developed may result in years of litigation.

Richard W. O'Neill believes it is important to know whether an existing or a contemplated land-use agency controls or seeks to control the land. O'Neill cites the following critical areas of land control:

- Beaches or beach fronts
- Flood plains
- Recreational areas
- Major transportation facilities (or proximity, to same)
- Land used for regional benefit
- Large-scale industrial developments
- Large residential developments (such as new towns)

Moreover O'Neill believes it is important to know if building over or directly adjacent to natural or man-made lakes and streams is restricted.

The National Flood Insurance Act, passed late in 1973, limits any community development on a 100-year, flood-plain area. However, in certain areas of the nation along the gulf coast of Texas and in southern Florida, insurance restrictions, such as Federal Housing Administration (FHA) restrictions on building below a 14-foot elevation above sea level, must be waived if any construction is to be permitted.

Voters were given an opportunity to express their views as to how land in one state should be developed in November 1972, when Californians were asked to approve or to reject Proposition 20, the controversial coastline protection initiative. Voter reaction was a significant way of letting legislators and public officials know the importance that their constituents placed on environmentalism.

Today almost every state has enacted or is considering enacting legislation to further expand its authority in the regulation of land use. California, Delaware, Maine, New Jersey, Rhode Island, and Washington exercise particularly broad state authority over land developments on or near the coast.

Connecticut, Georgia, Maryland, Massachusetts, North Carolina, and Virginia have singled out wetlands for jurisdiction. Each of these states requires a permit for any draining, dredging, filling, or construction in these areas.

Minnesota, Michigan, and Wisconsin have enacted strong shoreland and flood-plain protection laws. Colorado, Florida, New Hampshire, New York, Oregon, Vermont, Utah, and Wyoming have also passed strong environmental protection and land-use laws. In almost every state the legislation was approved because it was considered to be in the best interests of the public.

CALIFORNIA'S PROPOSITION 20

In 1975 California's Coastal Zone Conservation Commission, in adopting its final statewide findings and policies, called the long-term goal of all coastal planning and development "the public ownership and access to a strip of land of varying width paralleling the coast." Specifically, the Commission stated: "The long-term goal of coastal planning and development should be to make the maximum amount of shoreline available for public use and enjoyment. Access to the coast for persons of all income levels, all ages, and all social groups shall be the goal, consistent with the need to protect coastal areas from destructive overuse and to protect both public rights and the rights of property owners."

The Commission emphasized that new development should be restricted to inland portions of existing coastal communities, where public transportation and other services are available, and that "new development shall not be permitted to sprawl, project by project, into open space."

The Commission did encourage recreational development for visitors, including resorts, restaurants, and campgrounds, but recommended prohibiting new developments from blocking seaward views from key public viewing points.

Those who have been most critical of the Commission's recommendations have been seriously and economically affected. One large landowner, unable to obtain permission to subdivide a portion of a 2000-acre rural parcel into 20-acre ranchettes, compared the power of the Commission to the forceable acquisition of private land for placement in public trust at the expense, in terms of the cost of the land carry, of the private owner.

However, California's Commission recently recommended that specific lands be acquired by state or local communities for the benefit of the public. Value would be determined by independent appraisal.

According to Sanford R. Goodkin, the smaller, local landholder may be developing a piece of land that literally represents his economic life or death. "Therefore he will pay very conscientious attention to it," Goodkin explains. "The smaller developer can be influenced to do a better job because of the economic necessities of that piece of land."

COMPENSATION FOR DEVELOPMENT RIGHTS

Private interests do not necessarily have to suffer economic losses because a government agency feels land in open space is for the benefit of the public. An excellent example is the program advocated by John V. N. Klein shortly after his election in 1971 as County Executive for Suffolk County, Long Island, New York. The plan was to have become operational in 1976.

In an effort to preserve the rural character of Suffolk County and its quality farmland and agricultural productivity, the county legislature voted $60 million in 30-year bonds to acquire development rights to compensate a farmer for potential loss of property value. For example, if a farm is worth $7000 an acre to a developer but only $2000 an acre as farmland, Suffolk County would pay the difference of $5000 an acre to the farmer, who must agree to keep the land in farmland forever.

The Suffolk County Agricultural Advisory Committee recommended that available funds be used to acquire development rights instead of fee title. When the county did acquire fee title, the Committee recommended that prior to considering a leaseback, the County should offer to sell the agricultural title to other commercial farmers on an open, competitive-bid basis.

Further, the Committee recommended that the first offer to purchase development rights should include both farmer-owned and operated land and adjacent nonfarmer-owned land. The preserved farms should constitute relatively large tracts, preferably a minimum of 200 acres in size, and if possible the farms should be bounded by existing roads, a highway, or some other open space to provide a buffer zone between the farm and any nearby residential or commercial properties.

The Committee pointed out in its report of March 1974 that whereas the purchase of development rights is of great benefit to the farmer, it also provides enormous benefits to the people of Suffolk County, both now and in the future, through the preservation of a vital industry and extensive open space. The report also stated that the concept of development rights permits the retention of ownership, possession, and maintenance of the property with the landowner, who, through the pride of ownership and possession, can be far more effective than the County in maintaining the physical condition of the property.

Suffolk County also created a Select Committee on the Acquisition of Farmlands to solicit bids and to make the final determination as to where development rights would be acquired.

This precedent-setting program, the first of its kind in the nation, when operational, could make it possible for landowners in other areas of the country who are currently restricted from developing land to require local government or public-interest groups to acquire the property at a fair market value, or to adequately compensate the owner, or to allow development. The program also could provide the community and its citizens with an opportunity to preserve open spaces and to maintain the character of their environment.

UNDERSTANDING THE ENVIRONMENTALIST

It is essential that any landowner or user understand the objectives of leading environmental groups and communicate with these groups to achieve a compromise if any disagreement arises. It is often in the best interests of opposing groups to resolve matters themselves, because time and effort spent in months or years of litigation represent costs that could be avoided by private negotiation.

Perhaps the most noted, quoted, and applauded conservation and environmentally oriented group is The Sierra Club. It also may be the most maligned, misunderstood, and abused of all as well. Michael McCloskey, Executive Director of The Sierra Club clarifies the Club's objectives:

Landowners who in one instance may reap the economic windfall benefits of suddenly being permitted to make a more economical, advantageous use of their land, also have to bear the speculative risk of having uses to which they hope to put the land curtailed by public regulation. What public regulation can give, it can take away.

Life and conditions constantly change, and any investor in land must run the risk of dealing with the exigencies of the real and changing world. The Sierra Club has no interest in trying to solve the problems of land investors and speculators. However, I do not think our policies are in any way inconsistent with a legitimate role for private investors in developments that are needed on private land under proper controls and plans. If investors want certainty in terms of government regulation, they could just as reasonably ask for certainty in the rate of return on their investment, and builders likewise in having their prices fixed by their suppliers. In short, this is an illusion and unreasonable supposition.

Until we can get developers and environmentalists and local authorities together on a more comprehensive and stable approach to planning, we are going to be locked in to an ad hoc kind of skirmishing.

Planning at the local level not only is usually fragmentary, but in large, metropolitan regions it deals just with one subunit of the region. It becomes impossible in that framework to figure out the interrelationship between the flow of population and the community and do any meaningful kind of comprehensive planning. This is one of the reasons environmentalists are so strongly behind proposals for national land-use legislation and encouraging states to do more comprehensive planning on a regional basis, as opposed to local-arena decision making and planning.

It is in the public interest to have urbanization occur in higher densities, largely within areas that already have been urbanized and in some cases within existing smaller communities. We do not think it is either efficient or desirable for sprawl to occur, where subdivisions are strung out in a long line in a helter-skelter manner along the coastline or in the mountain regions.

Generally speaking, we are increasingly opposed to more urban sprawl with single-family residences or light-density development at the periphery of existing urban areas. We think it is environmentally undesirable, because not only does it consume open space and in many instances valuable agricultural land, but it is inefficient in its use of energy. Such development requires long commutes, more freeways and road systems, and results in more water-pollution problems from storm-sewer runoff, deposits more smog, consumes more water, and is more expensive ultimately to the buyer.

We do want to see more high-density developments, which cluster multifamily dwellings and utilize bypassed lands. More effort should be concentrated in the redevelopment of rundown areas by rehabilitation of existing units.

We want something in between development of the urban periphery and the high-rise, high-density of the inner-city core. The type of development that has occurred in San Francisco, with a mix of townhouses and 15- or 20-story apartment buildings in cluster developments near centers of commerce strikes us as reasonably attractive.

On the whole there are advantages to dealing with larger developers in that they can construe their interests in a broader sense to respond to planning over hundreds of miles of area. The smaller, local developer has only an option to build and develop very close to home or not do it at all.

Sanford R. Goodkin believes that many builders have not used land in a sensitive manner in the past:

Somewhere between the necessity for open areas, parks, and allowing "Mother Nature" to nurture her children, and the basic economic necessities of the developer, be he large or small, there will evolve a relationship between the environmentalists and the users of land to do a sensitive job, providing housing, buildings, and other uses that are necessary for the sociological and cultural growth of our society.

COMMUNICATING WITH ENVIRONMENTALISTS

Michael McCloskey believes that any wise developer should want to know the possible situations he may have to face. "This involves looking at whether or not there is an active environmental movement in his community," McClosky explains. "He should make contact with them and see what things are most precious and important to them."

McCloskey's views are reaffirmed by a number of leading land developers and builders who want to know and understand the reasons for any opposition to their plans. Louis E. Fischer notes:

We are always wide open for reasonable discussion. We try to work with local environmental groups, because we want them to know our objectives and we want to know their wishes. Once we sit down and discuss the plans, we find our mutual interests are not that diverse. We want to build a viable community, and that generally is the same thing they want. Those who believe you shouldn't build anything at all are being unrealistic in this world today.

Of course, there were a number of cases where many well-meaning people became involved in situations they did not understand, and by lack of understanding, even with their good intent, became responsible for some irresponsible actions. However, I do believe the worst is over, because those who have lasted in the pursuit of these interests probably are the more responsible individuals. And their actions were brought about because of a number of builders and developers who did perform irresponsible acts.

Irwin Adler complains that in many sensitive areas no growth advocates use ecology and the environment as excuses to prevent development. "They are opposed to the project, because they are selfish and want no development," he feels.

Adler's views were supported by McCloskey of The Sierra Club:

In the profusion of ad hoc environmental groups that have formed across the country in the past few years, there may be a certain number of them who really are nothing more than neighborhood associations that have chosen some environmental name and may claim they are a local league to protect the environment of such and such a city or neighborhood.

No one can really tell from a national point of view how many such groups there may be or how bona fide they are. But it can lead to confusion about who is an environmentalist.

When such situations arise, it is important for the developer or builder to ask how long the organization has been in existence; what bona fide environmental projects of any consequence the organization has been involved in; what its track record has been; and what its overall program is. Those questions can and should be asked, because actions on a local level only confuse the public about what is and is not really being done to protect the environment.

PETALUMA: THE CASE FOR LOCAL CONTROL

Petaluma, California, once strictly an egg-ranching center, is located 40 miles North of San Francisco in Sonoma County. During the 1960s

Petaluma became one of the fastest-growing suburbs in the San Francisco metropolitan area, and by 1970 its population had almost doubled.

In 1972, after studying the rate and pattern of the town's growth for the previous 20 years, during which the population had tripled, and for the previous two years, during which the city had approved the construction of twice as many housing units as it had approved in the two prior years, the Petaluma City Council became alarmed and adopted guidelines to slow the rate of future development. The guidelines were approved in a citywide referendum.

The Petaluma Plan established a growth rate for the city that was not to exceed 500 subdivision housing units per year; set a maximum population for the city in 1985; drew a property line to define the outer limits of the city's physical growth for 20 years; and established an environmental design plan.

The 500-unit housing limitation applied only to projects involving five or more units. Petaluma's growth was to be controlled by establishing a 200-foot-wide greenbelt around the city as a boundary expansion for the next 5–15 years. Growth outside the greenbelt would be restricted by the city's refusal to extend water and sewer facilities.

On April 24, 1973, the Construction Industry Association of Sonoma filed suit against the city of Petaluma, asking that the plan be declared unconstitutional. In January 1974 the U.S. District Court ruled that the Petaluma Plan violated the right to travel guaranteed by the Constitution, when a permanent injunction was issued against the city's attempt to restrict growth.

Judge Lloyd H. Burke ruled that a town is obligated to construct public utilities to meet a population level that is set by "market and demographic growth rates" and that "a solution both real and practical ... is for increasing the capacity of the existing sewage treatment plants." Local home-builder groups and numerous civil rights and antiexclusionary zoning groups had supported the action to seek the injunction.

The Sierra Club and the Natural Resources Defense Council filed a friends-of-the-court brief in October 1974 in the U.S. Court of Appeals in support of the city's right to govern its development. The environmentalists' brief stated that this case stood at a critical juncture in the history of land use and environmental planning. Michael R. Sherwood, attorney seeking the appeal, stated:

Since World War II urban sprawl has been underway, and both citizen and government task forces have been calling for the formulation and adoption of new techniques to ensure that the impact of growth on the environment is minimized through careful land-use planning.

The District Court decision effectively ends the freedom of local and regional government to work for growth regulation. The alternative is unregulated growth, earmarked by overcrowding; unsightly and unhealthy urban sprawl; a dangerous overtaxing of municipal services, such as water and sewage disposal; and a general lowering of the quality of life as open space disappears and excessive noise and air pollution multiply.

Sherwood stressed that the environmentalists "emphatically deplore" the fact that local land-use regulation has too often been applied with the intent and effect of excluding low-income and minority segments of the population from residence in environmentally more pleasing areas and stated that growth-regulating ordinances need not and should not have this effect. "Opening up the suburbs to the poor is one thing; having the suburbs open to the unchecked discretion of developers is quite another," Sherwood concluded.

On August 13, 1975, in a unanimous three-member decision, the Ninth U.S. Circuit Court of Appeals upheld the legality of the Petaluma Plan, reversing Judge Burke's earlier decision. Circuit Judge Herbert Y. C. Choy wrote: ". . . The concept of the public welfare is sufficiently broad to uphold Petaluma's desire to preserve its small-town character, its open spaces, and low density of population, and to grow at an orderly and deliberate pace."

Other California cities voted funds to help Petaluma fight the litigation. Many courts in California and throughout the United States have enacted similar growth-control laws in recent years in an effort to reduce the environmental deterioration brought on by rapid expansion and the burdens it places on taxpayers to provide new city services.

At the time of the landmark decision city officials noted that since the adoption of the Petaluma Plan no permits had been denied builders of single-family homes or of structures up to four units unless they were part of larger development projects.

The final legal decision has upheld the legality of the Petaluma Plan.

MORE DECISIONS, DECISIONS

Another landmark decision establishing that government, not the marketplace, should control municipal growth was made in the New York Court of Appeals in 1972 in *Golden v. Planning Board of Ramapo, N.Y.*

Like Petaluma, the town of Ramapo was a rapidly expanding suburban area located within commuting distance of New York City. The town was faced with urban sprawl and leapfrog development, where builders were bypassing open land close to the center of a city to develop less expensive land farther out.

Leapfrog development has been criticized because it pushes housing beyond the limits of existing municipal services and places the burden for increasing and extending new services directly on the town's taxpayers. To prevent such development, the town of Ramapo amended its zoning ordinance, making the right to subdivide a plot a special land use that required a special permit to build. A point system was created to rate the number and distance of municipal services from a proposed building site. The plan automatically prevented many owners of land on the outskirts of Ramapo from developing their property. To avoid appearing confiscatory, the town added an 18-year capital improvement program to its new zoning ordinance to extend municipal services throughout the town. As a result no developer would have to wait more than 18 years for enough points to permit subdivision and development of his property.

The ordinance was challenged, and the New York State Supreme Court upheld the town's right to control municipal growth based on its ability to provide water and sewage lines. The court ruled that although "timing" controls were not specifically authorized by state legislation, they were "necessarily implied" by the municipality's power to restrict and regulate land use.

The significance of the Ramapo and Petaluma cases is that they have inexorably pitted the issue of an "individual's right to travel" against the government's right to regulate land use.

However, in the spring of 1974 the U.S. Supreme Court, in *Borass v. Village of Belle Terre,* upheld the right of the town of Belle Terre to adopt a zoning ordinance that restricts future land use to single-family dwellings and virtually ensures that the town will not grow larger than its present population of 700. Writing for the majority, then Justice William O. Douglas upheld that it is a legitimate exercise of the police power of the state for a locality to adopt a zoning ordinance, adding: "A quiet place where yards are wide, people are few, and motor vehicles are restricted are legitimate guidelines in a land-use project. . . ." Justice Douglas chose to ignore the arguments of the plantiffs that the Belle Terre zoning ordinance "interferes with a person's right to travel."

Despite the Belle Terre ruling, one of the first zoning cases to reach it in years, the U.S. Supreme Court still maintains an obscure position on zoning.

OTHER POLITICAL RISKS

"If you buy a large piece of land that is going to take three or four years to develop, and there are controversial proposed uses, you could have a different city council or a different board of supervisors who could decide to rezone the land and totally wipe you out," says Ronald R. Foell. "The risks in the political arena are much greater now than they ever were in the past. This increases the risk when you are holding land for a long period of time and it is essential that before closing the transaction the buyer has all municipal approvals."

Foell cites one instance where a local government suddenly determined that the sewer plant was over capacity and imposed a building freeze, even on improved lots. "This was a disaster for many large builders who held large acreage and a significant number of improved lots. Suddenly millions of dollars in land became valueless."

Sewer moratoriums may be effective in communities where no surrounding land is available. However, this action can prove counterproductive when a local government forces developers to seek alternative areas even farther outside the municipality, where septic tanks are allowed or where the developer installs his own treatment system and adds the cost to the selling price of the house.

Another means of controlling land use is employed in Stockholm, Sweden. There the municipality controls all the surrounding property, because land is usable only if it is accessible to transportation courses to the central city. The municipality controls highway development and an efficient rapid transit system. City planners determine what land is to be developed, for what specific use, and when. Only then is the land made accessible to transportation routes.

Deed restrictions were the only method of zoning in the United States for a number of years. When George Washington lived at Mount Vernon, lands were conveyed by the Crown of England. As a rule the stipulation of transfer meant that the owner must fulfill certain requirements before he could pass his land along to the next owner. People who subsequently subdivided the land wrote restrictive covenants into every deed that were often much worse than municipal zoning requirements. Over time, however, many deed restrictions and some discriminatory zoning proved perishable, being ruled unconstitutional or not in the best interests of the public.

Technicalities, interpretations, moratoriums, injunctions, delays, and litigation only add costs for the final improvement. The public must pay, either directly or indirectly, for the controls it exercises over land use. If land is to be acquired for public use at a fair market rate from private interests, then the public must pay directly by voting for bond issues and supporting the acquisition through increased taxes. Delays that increase carrying costs, the costs of reports and studies to justify land improvement, are indirectly passed on to the public in the form of higher costs for housing, for services and entertainment at resorts and recreational facilities, and even for electricity when utilities have difficulty obtaining approval for new facilities.

CHAPTER XI

INCREASING LAND VALUES

From the first building boom after World War II until the 1970s, a landowner had to do little or nothing to realize a profitable gain on the sale of land. Land prices almost automatically escalated annually, and throughout the country it was a seller's market.

Even in a period of recession and tight money, selected parcels of land are salable if the location is right, the demand is present, and the necessary approvals can be obtained from government agencies. Some landowners can turn a profit in a matter of months. Profit opportunities can also be maximized by creating demand for land. Making an effort to improve its value can produce a more viable and marketable property that may return an even greater profit than the same piece of land with no improvements.

Professionals in the real estate industry have different reactions to increasing land values. Some of these include:

- Change the permitted use of the property by rezoning.
- Build improvements into the property to increase land value.
- Utilize public relations and advertising to create a demand for the land if it has a strong, marketable identity.
- Develop a plan to make the land profitably developable and buildable.
- Create a demand through land control.

Each of these concepts may be successful in some market areas and not necessarily as successful in others or even in the same market area

102

under different conditions. Before deciding which approach to take, the landowner should carefully evaluate professional market research to determine the most profitable use for his property. Market research is a vitally important factor in choosing the course of action to follow.

CHANGING THE PERMITTED USE OF THE PROPERTY

Generally, the value of land is increased by changing its permitted use from farming to residential, or from residential to commercial, or by creating a greater density and then selling or developing the land. This is usually accomplished by rezoning, but in most instances today additional approvals from environmentally oriented government and quasi-government agencies are also required.

"The people who are professionals in land look to rezone," says William E. Becker. "The way money is made in land is not to use it for the use it was originally intended, but rather to rezone it and give it its highest investor use."

But zoning does not always mean creating a higher density for the project. Zoning also can be *down*-zoning, changing the use from commercial to residential, or from multifamily to single-family housing. William Phillips of Phillips, Brandt and Reddick, Inc., believes that today lower density in most given markets has a better chance of selling. "The first problem to overcome is to convince the client that you do not have to get the highest density to be profitable. High density only costs time and money in getting approvals. For example, take a piece of land and assume it is a foregone conclusion that it will be developed someday. If the owner has the time to wait for urban growth to reach that property and the financial means to carry it, the land most likely could be developed at traditional community density. However, by developing the land now at a lower density there can be more immediate profit to the owners. Unless the holding costs are turned around, it really won't make any difference what density is approved for the property."

Barry A. Berkus, Santa Barbara architect and planner, believes zoning ordinances must remain pliable:

As community needs change, new concepts of land use are dictated within its borders to guarantee continuing liability.

Furthermore, environmental pollution requirements and transportation technology are necessitating further reevaluation of existing land-use policies in the urban core.

There have been some disastrous mistakes made in the past that hopefully will not happen in the future. Builders who hopscotched land and put high-density projects prematurely on open farmland created false land values and accelerated development, causing many of the problems developers face today with environmentalists. While the project may have been profitable for the builder, it was not in the best interests of planned community development, and with a density of 12–14 units an acre instead of 4, land values jumped from $5000 an acre to $20,000 an acre.

Ideal planning concepts have been rendered invalid by projects of too large a scale. The definition of scale remains the weak link in the equation of longevity.

We just have not learned from the Europeans. So many great villages remain valid living environs forever because of an understanding of scale that results in a strong aesthetic statement. We've overlooked this village-type concept all too often in our new communities and particularly in so many destination resorts.

On the other hand, with new services and amenities being created in the inner city, a new demand will be created where people will want to live and work in the same vicinity. The urban core can be renovated, so land stops deteriorating in value, stabilizes in price, and can actually increase in value. The key is a transportation system that must be created to move people within the urban core, as well as to and from the urban core.

William Phillips regards the planned community concept as an effective zoning tool. "I believe getting a piece of property zoned as a planned community, which encompasses many different uses, helps an owner enrich the value of his land. This places a greater guarantee on the land. It is a clear prediction of what the land will be like at ultimate development, whereas zoning in too many instances is just cutting it up in small pieces.

"The planned community allows the convenient mix of land uses in proportion to whatever the desire or the need is of the whole plan. It allows the developer to introduce innovations that might otherwise not be possible. It takes into consideration the total regional approach to planning, rather than a site-by-site approach," Phillips says.

ENHANCING LAND VALUES THROUGH IMPROVEMENTS

When a parcel of raw land is serviced by essential utilities or improved by development, its value increases. A residential community creates commercial value for a shopping center location, because the new residents need to buy groceries, drugs, clothes and services.

"Land sitting out in the middle of nowhere with nothing happening depreciates in value, and at the luckiest stays the same," says Ralph Shirley. "People, traffic, construction, and activity create the values for land.

"I don't make money selling the first builder the first 100 or 200 acres, but I do make money selling the next 10, 20, or 30 acres once he has started building something. That is the key to getting appreciation in value."

Barry A. Berkus emphasizes the need for continuity. "Large companies previously involved in the retail sale of land must make the transition to development to build value into the land they have sold and still have to sell," Berkus adds. "These companies have a responsibility to their customers and to themselves to guarantee a continuity of sensitive development, ensuring the value of the land that has been sold in the past and the land they will be selling in future years."

Paul T. Pohly believes single-family housing should be constructed first to create a neighborhood environment. "You start building atmosphere. You reserve your best land for multifamily development, whether attached sales housing or rental apartments, and for commercial development. These parcels will increase in value once the new demand has been created," he says.

Recreational amenities are a way to create an immediate atmosphere and to set the stage for future development in a new community. Depending on the size of the project, amenities can include golf, tennis, a man-made lake, or a country club.

William Nolan points out that a large, new community project in which the builder converted a 22-acre parcel into a lake became the focal point for the recreational facilities. Nolan explains:

The cost of the land plus the lake was $300,000, which was built into the cost of future lot sales to builders. We took the position that the land values immediately surrounding the country club and lake were greater than those not immediately surrounding them, and phased development and sales there accordingly.

The key to the marketing effort was that the country club was to become a self-supporting profit center. Membership at first was not limited to just those who lived in the community, but to all in the area. The nonresidents were attracted to the community and eventually many became buyers.

While there are pros and cons regarding the capital investment in front-end amenities, often it is more advantageous than paying for a bond to guarantee that eventually the recreational amenities will be built. And all the time they are working for you, increasing your land values.

CREATING DEMAND THROUGH PROMOTION

William Phillips believes that an effective promotional campaign can appreciate the value of a piece of property, either by associating it with another successful project or by creating a marketable image for it. Phillips advises:

> Success breeds success. An address or association with one community versus another can make a big difference in the property values, even though one could drive through and look at both areas, not noticing any appreciable difference.
>
> If you have a remote land holding that is really not associated with anything, then research the history of the property. Find out if there is anything unique about the land. Perhaps some explorer passed through it. Every place has some history, and all you have to do is research it, document the facts, and then capitalize on it through public relations and advertising.
>
> Some properties have many unnamed creeks. Name them. If a creek should be named, for example, John Jones Creek, find out who John Jones was, and capitalize on this.

Romantic and historic associations with a piece of land can create consumer appeal. A public relations and advertising program can be built around this concept. Such associations should be projected in publicity releases, collateral materials, sales displays, and advertising. Special events directly related to the romance and history of the project can be arranged to bring traffic to the site.

Ask a history professor from a nearby high school or university to research the property. Being an expert in his field, his documented facts will probably not be challenged.

In some instances land may have no historic value, and a completely creative advertising approach is necessary. A theme or an association with advantages that will appeal to the end user can be created for a new community. Market research analysis can define and assess the demographic appeals to the end user, and an advertising program can be directed to this segment of the public.

DEVELOPING A WORKABLE PLAN FOR LAND USE

Planning the use of the land is essential for a large project, whether or not the owner ever intends to develop the property. A plan for development increases the salability of the land, because it shows a potential buyer the opportunities inherent in developing the property.

"The planner must understand what will be acceptable to the local community," advises Robert Martin Engelbrecht. "The timing for a piece of land also is important, because needs and demands change. One must realize that you do not have to develop every square foot of land, but in fact in many instances it is better to develop less initially and leave more in a land bank that will return an even greater yield later. Most land appreciation in this country occurs without any rezoning at all. It occurs just due to the pressure of demand for land as valued land."

Engelbrecht cites the example of a project in which the developer was losing $100,000 a year because he had no master plan for development. "The nucleus of the entire program was a village, but because of traffic on weekends, it sometimes took people 45 minutes to drive the last three miles into the village. The village itself had problems with its accommodation and service facilities. The master plan created a better traffic flow and made the village a more acceptable destination for people. The area around the village was planned for eventual use. When the master plan was finished and approved, the company eventually was able to sell its interest in the village for three times what they originally started to sell it for," he said.

Kenneth W. Agid believes planning includes accommodating social change and every element of life, including consumer needs and wants. "Value is created by planning in front of the users as long as 15 years, by anticipating and projecting the needs of the consumer and preplanning those uses on the land," Agid states.

But planning entails more than developing a master plan for the land. Planning is the act of making the property more developable and buildable. This means overcoming obstacles. William Phillips suggests:

Take a piece of land isolated in terms of major access points that is not even a member of a major water district or sanitation district, is two or three miles from a major water supply line, has no connection rights to any sewage treatment facilities, and is in an unincorporated area.

You must work out priorities to get the extension of the water lines to the sites throughout the area. That is not zoning, but just pure bonding and priority assessment. Next, work out an on-site sanitation treatment facility on an interim basis to supply half the project with treatment. Overcome the sewage problem by developing your own system, with a future commitment to hook onto other municipal lines. Next, create a low-intensity phase-development program, so little burden is placed on the transportation system for the near term. These three items were keys to escalating the land value in an area with no development.

If you have commitments to water-supply and commitments to treatment-facility connections, the value of the land will increase.

CREATING DEMAND BY LAND CONTROL

Often land values are successfully increased by exercising control over adjacent parcels or marketable parcels to place similar types of improvements on the land.

William E. Becker cites the case of a successful builder who optioned every parcel of land in his market area that could conceivably be zoned. The options were for one year. Becker states:

The builder's project was successful, because there was no competition in the marketplace. Projects were begun on land that had zoning approval, and at the end of the option period the builder let the options expire. By this time, his competition was a year or more behind in trying to penetrate the market, had to pay considerably more for the land, and through normal escalation of wages and materials, found it difficult to produce a comparable product at a competitive price.

Barry A. Berkus explains:

Ambient air quality standards may reverse our past conceptual process of locating high-density commerce centers near major freeway intersections. Land in such a location has historically been considered high value for such use. However, we now cannot build major shopping centers near freeways, not only because of the air pollution from the freeways, but because of the slow moving, high-pollution traffic within the complex. Such land will best be utilized for lower density.

The future will be in village-type or neighborhood shopping centers that do not create high-traffic density, where people are transported by a flexible, soft-wheel transit system such as minibuses. As transportation needs and patterns change, such a system is flexible as opposed to a fixed rail system. Such a concept further allows for change in development around the village, and the traffic flow can quickly adapt to the changing population patterns of the area.

Planners must not be fixed in their concepts and approach to land use. For example, the mobile module developed during the 1970s offered a sound method of retaining land in an unsubdivided state that allowed interim bedroom communities to fill the void of low- and moderate-income housing until the best use could be determined for that land. The interim use allowed the landowner to offset the carrying cost of the land while it improved in value and the development process around it occurred.

The fear of control by a government agency and the ongoing burden of the carrying costs has pressured some people into development that should not have taken place. This is particularly true in areas very sensitive to environmental groups, such as along seacoasts.

Such land is very desirable and, of course, limited in supply. This is land that should not be down-zoned, but very carefully and sensitively planned, creating the best lifestyle and amenity pattern dictated by the natural amenities, geography, and availability of resources. Done properly, high density cannot be considered a negative development approach, as there always will be demand for good projects in such locations.

Owners, fearing their land values may be rendered worthless, have rushed to create some type of development to protect their investment. By understanding planning and government's willingness to be moderate, such parcels of land would have been utilized better with an interim project until the best use for that land could be determined.

The preplanning of new towns must take into consideration the natural resources available in yet undeveloped or lightly developed areas. This is one way to balance the burden now taxing our urban environs. Such planning must relate to the necessity of shifting new industrial or commercial centers to anchor the new developments, creating a viable economic base for the new town. Some of this can be achieved through lower tax bases or other incentives to entice business and industry to pioneer the move into the area. Without the economic base, the new town cannot become feasible or a reality.

CHAPTER XII

MARKETING AND SELLING THE LAND

Numerous concepts and techniques can be used to market and sell land. However, the objectives of the seller, which can be influenced by a number of factors beyond his control, first must be clearly defined.

A marketing and sales plan should be conceived by carefully weighing the variables that could affect the objectives of the seller, as well as those of the buyer. The sales and marketing effort can be as simple as posting a "For Sale" sign on the site or listing the property with a broker or sales agent; it can be as complex as a detailed, comprehensive plan that may be executed over a period of several years.

In developing the strategy to sell a piece of land, the prospective buyer must be identified. The seller should objectively analyze the land from the viewpoint of the buyer. Factors that help to categorize and identify the buyer by type or group include the location of the land, its potential end use, the size of the parcel, and its price.

• The *location* of the site is critical, because there are particular types of buyers for particular types of land. Inner-city land may appeal to one class of buyer; rural or resort land, to another.
• The *potential end use* of the land and whether or not it is zoned for that use further help to classify the prospective buyer. The developer of a shopping center would be no more interested in land suitable for a tract of 100 single-family homes than a suburban, residential builder-

developer would be in acquiring a downtown parcel for a high-rise office building.

• The *size* of the parcel further restricts the seller's market. A piece of land zoned and suitable for a neighborhood or a convenience shopping center may be too small to interest a company that specializes in large-scale, regional shopping centers. A small, residential builder who averages 50 new housing starts a year would not be considered a prospective buyer for a parcel of land to accommodate a 400-home tract with an annual absorption rate of 125 units. The size of the parcel being sold is important to a buyer today due to environmental influences. Development cycles have been shortened, and many astute professionals currently consider only projects in which there is a quick turnover of the land and product.

• The *price* that the seller hopes to obtain for the land and the terms and conditions that are acceptable in a sale also help to identify the type of buyer. Some prospects may not have the necessary capital, net worth, borrowing capacity, or financial resources to purchase certain parcels. The higher the asking price, the more limited the market. The seller must ask himself: Is the asking price a fair market price? Am I willing to earn a lower profit? Am I willing to take a loss to sell the land? How can the sales transaction be structured to best meet my investment and tax-planning objectives? How quickly do I want to sell the land? What asking price will result in a quick sale? Is there actually a demand for this type of land? How real is the demand?

The seller must also recognize that the marketability of land can be affected by conditions that are beyond his control. Influential factors may include:

• General economic conditions locally, regionally, or nationally that would directly affect the demand for particular types of land.

• Economic conditions in the real estate industry itself; whether the land is suited for a particular type of improved development that could be either overbuilt or badly needed.

• The general availability of similar parcels of land in location, size, end-use potential, and price.

• The aggressiveness of environmental groups, and the influence they could assert to obtain necessary zoning or down-zoning of the property.

• The past performance of local government officials in expediting land development approvals, and the attitudes of elected officials toward new growth and development in the community.

• The availability of the utilities necessary for land development, including sewer, water, and power.

• The tax base and structure of taxation in the community as an advantage or a deterrent.

• The availability to potential buyers of financing from local lenders.

DEVELOPING THE PLAN

When conceptualizing the marketing and selling approach, the seller should consider every advantage and disadvantage of the property, just as if he were evaluating the land for acquisition.

In any public offering and in most interstate sales of land, either in syndication of medium and large parcels or in retail lot sales, full disclosure of all pros and cons of the property must be made in a written prospectus. Whether required by law or not, it is always wise for the seller to be factually accurate when making any claims about the land, because any misrepresentation of the property could result in a recision of the sale.

A builder or developer who acquires land for his own eventual use or for sale to the consumer should have already conceived a marketing plan before consummating the land transaction. This plan may be prepared by the company's staff or by a competent professional consulting firm. Whether the land is intended to be used for a small office building, an industrial park, a new town, interim development, or whatever, the seller should construct a written plan for marketing and selling the land.

Similarly, an individual, private investor should define objectives for marketing and selling land before an acquisition is made, even if the plan is only stated in one sentence. Investment objectives can change, depending on the length of time land is held. Because of the ever-changing factors that influence land marketability and value, the seller's marketing and selling plan should be sufficiently flexible to be adaptable to current economic, sociological, and environmental trends and conditions.

A BASIC APPROACH

For whatever type of land he is marketing, even if it is only one small, residential lot, the seller should prepare an information or fact sheet containing the fundamental information a buyer would normally request. Such a fact sheet should include:

• Location of the property, described with mailing address or streets bounding the site that can be located on available maps.

- Legal description of the property.
- The zone use for the land.
- Comment regarding potential use of the land.
- Description of surrounding parcels of land, improved or unimproved.
- Real estate taxes, including dollar figures, assessed valuation by the tax assessor, and the tax rate for the current fiscal year (if projected, estimated taxes should be included). The last time (month and year) the property was appraised should also be recorded.
- Information and data of market research interest to a prospective buyer, based on end-use potential, describing surrounding amenities, advantages, and reasons that may be important to the buyer. This should include a description of the general surrounding area: road access; distance in miles and average driving time to freeway ramps, shopping centers, public transportation, schools, churches, and so on; possible environmental restrictions, either local or federal, that could affect the issuance of building permits; and liens on the property, including first and second trust deeds, if any.
- The company name, address, telephone number, and, if possible, the individual to be contacted to secure each utility service: telephone, water, sewer, gas, and electricity.
- Whether financing is available, and if there is a commitment from a lending institution or from the seller.
- The sales or asking price. The terms and conditions of sale should be included, if they can be disclosed. It is important to state if the land is for sale or lease.
- The name, address, and telephone number of the seller, sales agent, or broker is most important. If the agent is willing to share the commission with other brokers, this should be stated. If the seller agrees to deal only with principals and for whatever reason is unwilling to pay a commission, this should be stated.
- Whether there are oil or mineral rights, and especially if these rights are or are not included in the sale or lease.

The basic information that should be disclosed in a fact sheet can easily be typed on one or two pages. Duplication costs, depending on the quantity of sheets desired, may be minimal; copies of the original fact sheet can be made on a photocopier in a library, a drug store, or even a supermarket for 10 cents apiece. The extent to which a presentation of the property or a marketing and sales program is to be implemented should be considered a cost factor in selling the property. Going one step further, the seller could also include the following in the sales information sheet:

- Photographs of the lot or parcel, the surrounding improvements, and

any key points that can be emphasized visually. These photographs do not need to be taken by a professional; they can be snapshots.
• A surveyor's report.
• A preliminary title report or abstract.

For any sale of consequential value, even one as inexpensive as $100,000, a brochure discussing the property should be prepared. This should be more than just an oil-company map with a circle pinpointing the location of the site. The brochure can be typewritten and reproduced either on a photocopying machine or by a specialty reproduction service. Ideally, the pages should be $8\frac{1}{2} \times 11$ in., or contained in such a format. A factual, professional presentation does not have to cost a lot of money.

Most stationery or office-supply stores carry the essential materials to prepare a brochure. If the sizes of some components of the brochure do not permit all the materials to be reduced to a standard $8\frac{1}{2} \times 11$ in. size, a preassembled presentation folder with pockets on the inside of the front and back covers can be purchased for about 30 cents. The basic information can be placed in one pocket; the supporting documentation, in the other. Plastic covers, plastic bindings, and other materials can also be purchased to give the presentation a professional appearance.

THE NEXT STAGE

Land sales for a new community or a new town, when a considerable amount of money is to be exchanged and when there are many potential buyers, should be prepared by or with the assistance or counsel of a professional company experienced in real estate transactions and marketing. This company could be a public relations firm, an advertising agency, or a marketing organization.

The sales presentation can be a one-color, two-color, or multicolor printed booklet. An audio-visual presentation in the form of 35-mm slides, a sound-slide filmstrip, or a movie can be prepared as a supplement to the printed booklet. The firm retained to counsel the presentation may even recommend an easel-card, flip-chart presentation, depending on the sales and profit goals of the seller.

The following information should be included in any comprehensive sales presentation:

• An aerial photograph of the property identifying all contiguous and important nearby parcels of land and significant points of reference.

- A topographical map.
- A report by an engineering or an architectural engineering firm, including charts and maps.
- Geological and soil reports, including charts and maps.
- All quantitative data that is available on request from utility companies, local chambers of commerce, local governments and redevelopment agencies, lending institutions, and commercial and industrial development organizations.
- An area map showing the specific locale of the property.
- Any correspondence from lending institutions, utilities, government agencies, or others regarding the property.
- Any newspaper or magazine articles of significant importance to the parcel of land.
- The name of the area. If the parcel to be sold is 10 out of 200 acres, the 10-acre site should be given a name in the presentation.
- Weather and climate in the area. A master plan of the site area, if made, including the map and all information prepared by the land planner.
- Labor supply and population demographics.
- Any independent market research that has been conducted.

MARKETING TO THE PROSPECT

Only after the preliminary sales presentation is complete and information about the land is compiled in a format the buyer can understand, should the seller make an effort to market the land to a prospect.

Site Sign. The least expensive marketing approach is the *site sign,* and this method may produce the best single response. The sign can be as simple as "For Sale" and a telephone number, or it can contain a detailed listing of the lot size, an outline giving the dimensions of the parcel, and zoning information. If the seller is paying an agent's commission, it is helpful to add the line "Broker Participation Welcome."

The Sales Agent. If the seller normally markets land on a general basis, he should contact certain brokers regularly to let them know what properties are available and on what terms the land can be sold. Sellers naturally have their favorite local brokers, but many sellers consider it bad policy to contact one agent exclusively. The agent's commission varies accordingly to the type of land being sold, the total sales price involved in the transaction, and a percentage of the initial cash payment.

The broker must secure prospective buyers and screen them to verify that they are qualified to purchase land. According to Sanford R. Goodkin, it is also the landowner's job to choose a sales agent or a sales team with an excellent track record that has integrity but that is aggressive enough to get the job done.

"In effect you will be speaking through their mouths and can get into trouble if they say things that are in violation of existing laws," says Goodkin. "Sales agencies all too often take the line of least resistance just to make the sale. That is how they make their living. It is important to keep them well trained, so that the law is laid down at the beginning that you will not tolerate any misrepresentation."

Lenders, Utilities, and Agencies.   Professionals who market and sell land provide the leading lending institutions involved in real estate transactions with information about their available properties. Buyers wishing to acquire land consult mortgage bankers, commercial banks, savings and loan associations, and thrift institutions to determine who to talk to in the local real estate market.

Sellers also should inform utility companies, industrial development commissions, chambers of commerce, and other local agencies about their available properties, particularly if the land they are marketing is suitable for commercial or industrial development.

Advertising.   Newspaper advertising can be an effective way of marketing land. Classified advertising is listed in the classified sections of the newspaper. Display advertising is usually no smaller than one column wide and one inch deep. Display rates are higher than classified advertising rates, but the seller can place a display advertisement in whatever section of the newspaper he chooses. For example, a display ad for resort acreage may produce a favorable response if it is placed in the sports section. Display ads for commercial or industrial land could be placed in the business/financial section of the newspaper. Classified and display advertising in selected trade publications, which reach specific audiences, also should be considered.

The seller should be realistic when advertising and should not spend the last dollar of a budget trying to totally capture a market. He should operate within a well-defined budget to generate funds for the advertising campaign.

"It is one thing to look at an ad when it is all by itself on a piece of paper, and quite another to see it reduced down to its true size in the classified or real estate sections of a newspaper," says Sanford R. Goodkin. "It diminishes in size almost automatically. Remember, any ad competes with other similar ads, and just an innovation of humor or a distinctive border can spell the difference between whether some potential buyer reads it or does not read it."

Direct Mail.   When the seller knows his prospective buyers personally, he should send a letter informing each buyer of the availability of the land. A similar letter, personally typed or robotyped by a mailing service, can then be mailed to identified but unknown prospects. Depending on the length of the seller's list of prospects, he must decide whether to include the cost of the sales presentation in his asking price. A self addressed postcard can be included in the letter for the prospect to return to request additional material, or the prospect can be given a telephone number to call collect.

For large mailings, firms that specialize in computer mailings can provide selective prospect lists. Personally signed and typed or robotyped letters generally elicit a greater response than a mailing in which the letter has been duplicated in mass and not personally signed. The most important consideration, however, is to identify the prospective buyer. No quantity of mailings will result in a sale if the letters are sent to people who are not at all interested in purchasing the land.

Sanford R. Goodkin advises that direct mail can hone in on a specific market segment that is qualified to buy a particular product. "However, direct mail is a very expensive medium to use, and the results can be very disappointing," Goodkin adds. "The mailing list is the difference between whether or not it will be effective. Check with a reputable mailing house to be certain you are not paying for an obsolete mailing list."

Conferences and Conventions.   Companies with large land holdings contract exhibit space at leading industry conferences and conventions to meet interested buyers personally. The sales effort then becomes a one-on-one approach in which questions can be quickly answered and the prospect's interest can be readily determined.

Information kits on available land parcels can be distributed on a selective or a mass basis, but the seller can assume that by virtue of exhibiting at an industry conference, a high percentage of the attendants are already prospects.

One company with large land holdings took an interesting approach at a major convention by distributing an information kit on available properties, with a letter explaining the terms and conditions of the sale. The letter stated:

At present, _____ does not price their land holdings. This may appear to be out of the ordinary, but as land holdings are vast and in several states, it is extremely difficult to keep pace with the current market values.

_____ does accept offers by: (1) receiving a letter of intent to purchase; (2) on receipt, the land is then appraised by an outside appraiser; (3) assuming the offer and appraisal are equal or close, _____ then proceeds to consider the offer and then to contract for the sale of the specific tract or tracts.

TERMS:

• 25% down; 8% of the 25% can be prepaid interest, but the interest must remain prepaid for the life of the note.
• _____ will consider a 10-year amortization, with a 5-year balloon on its smaller tracts and a 7-year balloon on the larger tracts.
• 8% interest.
• _____ does not issue a general warranty, but will give a special warranty deed and title policy (further clarification will be given, if desired).
• All offers must be approved by _____'s board of directors, and it reserves the right to specify the closing date.
• In most cases _____ does not own minerals, but there are exceptions. These will be specified on request.
• Financial statements are required on or before closing that must demonstrate the financial stability of the purchasers; this requirement holds true even if personal liability is not required.
• _____ prefers that their attorneys prepare the contracts; thus considerable time is saved.
• 5% escrow deposit is required with the submission of the letter of intent, unless otherwise specified and mutually agreed to by all parties involved previous to said submission.
• _____ has other requirements, but these will be explained on an individual basis.

The letter also stated that these requirements were intended only to be general guidelines and were subject to change or alteration without notice. The names, addresses, and telephone numbers of the appropriate individuals to contact were also contained in the letter.

SELLING THE PLANNED COMMUNITY

In marketing land in a planned community development or in a new town, it is very important for the seller establish the theme, image, and excitement of the development and then to control its design, growth, and lifetime.

As part of his marketing plan, the landowner may even set the stage by undertaking initial projects himself. Referring to a new community development in which he was involved, William Nolan states:

We did the first housing program, because we wanted to establish a trend from a design standpoint and to establish a quality standard to put the local citizen at ease.

The development was in an area near residences of extremely upper-income level people. We wanted them to be comfortable with our program. We built a 17-unit townhouse project with a homeowners' association, full security with a 24-hour guard, and had a $90,000 selling price. This immediately made the people living in $80,000 houses feel comfortable, because, if anything, we were improving their resale values. In fact, 12 of the units were sold to people who lived in the immediate neighborhood.

The second project was with a quality builder who was entering a new market. We put the land in at our cost, creating an operating company, and took a 50% position from an equity standpoint. The builder had no front-end costs, as he would have had entering the market without coming into a planned community such as ours.

Once the first builder was selling successfully, it made it easier for us to convince the next builder-prospect to buy land and to build in our community. At that point our program was off and running; we were getting profit on our joint venture and then began selling land at market value.

A typical transaction might be a 150-unit program with a projection of 50 units a year. Assume the package for the land was $500,000. The buyer paid us 20% down, or $100,000. We released 10% of that down payment for the equivalent number of lots he could take down, giving the builder-buyer his model homes and the start of his first production houses. After that, the builder-buyer would take down on a per-lot basis what he needed, making payment as he did.

Our contract was conditional on us getting the zoning, because if we were unable to get the zoning we wanted the land to revert to us.

Nolan states that once the master plan of a new community is finished, the seller should consult a builder organization that has a reputation for sophistication and good performance and the financial capability to start a program and to see it through to fruition. Nolan explains:

We sought out builders who were operating in other new towns or large PUDs. They had the understanding of what market research and services we would provide. We knew the housing demand in the area. We knew what type of housing would sell at what price range, and how much market penetration could be anticipated for a given product in a given price range.

As part of our marketing service, we introduced our buyers to local lenders in town and helped them establish a banking connection. We assisted them in any service area possible, even to the point of recommending local or regional interior decorators and advertising and public relations agencies. We even contracted for about half of the outdoor billboards in town and used them for our own institutional advertising campaign until such time as a builder was ready to do his own campaign. Then we sublet the billboards to him.

William Baker believes it is important for the seller to be responsible for all zoning and planning when marketing a new community. "We zone the land. We plan the land. We establish a liaison with every government agency that will in any way be involved with the property. And we hope we are able to do a better job than anybody else in the area and certainly better than anyone entering the market for the first time.

"The seller also builds the recreational facilities, the project amenities and the community themes," says Baker. "A complete development should be planned with land for every conceivable use: industrial, commercial, and all kinds of residential from the very expensive single-family lot to the least expensive townhouse lot."

Maintaining control over the type of development is as important to the buyer who is making a commitment to the project as it is to the seller who is seeking continued protection of land values.

Louis E. Fischer advocates leasing rather than selling land in community developments as a real means of exercising control. "We're looking very seriously at a number of lease opportunities for commercial and industrial properties," he said.

"This gives us the opportunity to control to a much greater extent what happens in those communities by virtue of our own efforts, our own development pace, and our own product design. We are an integral part of the community, so the continuing operational income from these entities is attractive to us where we are in a reasonable position of control. If we have an outright sale, we have lost control. And in the long term that could work against the interest of our community and our company."

"The difference between marketing and selling," according to Kenneth W. Agid, "is that marketing focuses on the needs of the consumer, whereas selling focuses on the needs of the seller. We think of ourselves as a viaduct or conduit for providing a service to the consumer.

"The consumer is looking for a product and it is our job to find out what that consumer wants and to provide it on a large scale. Land is worth only what the next user is willing to pay for the use provided him on the land or the use he can provide himself. The builder must understand what that next user wants and what he is willing to pay for it, and then residual back to what the land value is with that new use on it. By overbuilding a property you pass the equitable level of return on the land itself," says Agid.

Irwin Adler has developed a theory that applies to residential merchant builders. "I never want to build the last 100 units of any project in which we are involved. Sell the land to another builder, take a short profit, and get out," Adler advises.

A new community marketed not only to builders who are land buyers for various types of real estate projects but also to the end users of the improved properties. This involves a concerted institutional campaign to convince people that they should live and work in the community. An appeal must be created, and such an image can be greatly enhanced by a public relations effort.

If growth in the area normally occurs by attracting outside residents, then the campaign must be broad and far reaching enough to make potential new residents aware of the community before they relocate.

Events and attractions in keeping with the quality theme and image of the community can be effective tools in making people aware of its lifestyle and advantages. Advertising can also help to build traffic to the site, but oversell or factual misrepresentation of the property should be avoided, so that the potential end user is not disappointed with what he sees on his first visit.

MARKETING RETAIL LOTS

"Hard sell" is the ubiquitous philosophy in the predominant number of marketing programs for the retail sale of recreational and resort lots. Too many people have been "burned" and "taken" by a desert-lot purchase that they believed would become their "oasis" but that still remains barren, unimproved wasteland years later. Such misrepresentations have led to legislative action to protect the consumer. But few companies today adopt a "soft sell" approach, even after class-action litigation amounting to multimillion dollar settlements for some, and probes, inquiries, and civil actions filed by the Federal Trade Commission, the Office of Interstate Land Sales of the U.S. Department of Housing and Urban Development, and attorneys general of various states.

"Nothing turned on the ire of the environmentalist—and rightly so—more than recreational lot developers," believes Sanford Goodkin.

"They were irresponsible and insensitive to the needs of the community, the land, and even the people who were buying.

"Fortunately, most of those poor businessmen have been put out of business. The primary job of the selling organization was to get a captive audience, whether they packaged the potential buyer on an airplane or a golf course and got a feeling of obligation by feeding the prospect and then building an invisible cage of guilt around him in the event he tried to escape without buying a piece of the land."

The retail-lot marketing approach inaugurated the free junket, which enables the prospect to view the property. At one time flights were prevalent from Chicago and New York to Florida, Nevada, and Arizona, and from San Francisco, Seattle, and Los Angeles to the Southwest and the Sierra Nevadas. But people took advantage of these junkets, considering them free weekend vacations. Carefully and dutifully, they played their parts as prospective buyers but wisely made no purchases.

Primarily for economic reasons companies began to reduce the number of junkets from metropolitan cities to what promised to become the new and wonderful vacationland in the sun.

Federal and state laws specifically state what information must be disclosed to the prospective buyer and what sellers can and cannot advertise. However, the pressure exerted on the prospect by a sales representative in a one-on-one situation has changed very little. Salesmen have been known to quickly forget "loyalty" or the "buyer advantages" of one project and move "down the road" for as little as $5 more a month. Many salesmen are even categorized by their companies as the "blue-suede shoe" variety or total mavericks compared to sales agents who deal with commercial, industrial, or residential properties.

Goodkin believes the best protection a potential buyer of retail lots can have is a real knowledge of the prime developer's past performance and whether there have been any complaints against the selling organization. "The potential buyer should check with the local district attorney, the Federal Trade Commission, and the Better Business Bureau to see if any complaints have been filed," Goodkin warns.

A responsible developer should be extremely careful in selecting a sales organization and in monitoring sales personnel.

Some of the primary techniques used to market retail lots include:

• Free round-trip air transportation and an all-expense-paid junket from the prospect's city to the site of the sale.
• Massive direct mailings with reply postcards to prospects on selective computer listings.

• Follow-up telephone calls to prospects who are identified as potential buyers for any number of demographic reasons.
• Full-color advertising supplements and inserts in major metropolitan newspapers.
• Elaborate full-color brochures containing master plans and renderings of the proposed city.
• Radio and television advertising to show the scenic beauty of the development.
• Elaborate and extensive audio-visual presentations.
• Advertisements in travel and general-interest magazines.
• Publicity by newspaper and magazine travel editors.

Few states have taken the initiative to protect their residents that New York has. The office of the Attorney General of New York forcefully prosecutes violators of the state's registration act, one of the first in the country and probably a prototype for the Interstate Land Sales Act and for other state laws. In New York the seller must register any public offering of retail-lot sales with the New York Department of State and must obtain approval before initiating any sales effort. The Attorney General's office prosecutes violators of the registration requirements.

A prospective land buyer who is excluded from purchasing a lot because he is a resident of a particular state should not necessarily be suspicious of the seller for the lack of state approval. Some companies may not consider residents of that state to be primary or secondary prospects and therefore may not feel it is worth investing the executive time or the legal expense to become approved.

Other companies have developed techniques to successfully promote the image of a retail-lot sale development by staging events that gain national publicity and exposure. No one has a legal right to censure what a broadcaster may say or a newspaper or magazine journalist may write based on a news event or an occurrence at the location. Planned and executed by a professional public relations firm, a newsworthy event can do more to project the quality image of a development than millions of dollars of advertising. This is the subtle sell in which the buyer is encouraged to seek out the seller, rather than vice versa. This approach is most effective in a selective sales program where the buyer is identified demographically according to income group and where lot sales are primarily directed toward the "sophisticated investor" in the 50% or higher tax bracket. A company interested in marketing retail lots should retain the counsel of a marketing-oriented public relations firm that is experienced not only in real estate but in leisure entertainment as well.

More than the sale of any other type of land, the marketing effort for retail-lot sales must be conservative and well within the guidelines established by governing legal authorities. It is not only good business but smart business to ensure that the buyer is satisfied that the seller will stand behind his commitment and that no misunderstanding or wrongdoing can result in a recision of the sale. An attorney who once represented a company with a major sales program of retail lots reiterated during the era of consumer-protection legislation in the early 1970s that if the company had followed the guidelines later proposed by certain states and federal agencies, not only would the buyers have been happier but the company would have been more profitable.

What can result from a misunderstanding between seller and buyer happened to a leading U.S. industrial company that sold more than $360 million of recreational land in California and Nevada from 1967 until July 1972, when it announced it was discontinuing its sales program. At the same time the company announced a $200 million reserve for losses, most of which was intended to cover the cost of withdrawing from land sales. Subsequently, the company agreed to a settlement of nearly $60 million in lawsuits brought against the company or its subsidiaries charging misrepresentation in the sale of recreational lands in 20 developments. The suits included civil actions as well as class-action lawsuits filed in state and federal courts.

The actions charged that the company had not provided the recreational facilities it had promised. The suits also stated that the company had misrepresented the value and investment potential of the land; had given false information about the possibilities of subdividing or splitting the lots; and had failed to construct promised access roads and highways. The plaintiffs further charged that sales personnel had used two-way radios to imply that lots were selling fast.

During this period of time, California's Attorney General, Evelle Younger, called rural, second-home subdivisions "one of the major environmental and investment problems in California."

Any organization or individual involved in selling retail lots must retain not only the advice and counsel of a competent real estate attorney in the state in which the development is located, but in every state in which a sales effort may be made, as well as auditors and accountants, and an authoritative public relations firm with sound real estate experience.

CHAPTER XIII

ACCOUNTING FOR PROFIT RECOGNITION IN REAL ESTATE TRANSACTIONS

Until 1970 there were few universally accepted principles for real estate accounting. The only guidelines that did exist had been established by individual accounting firms for internal use and application to their own clients. These guidelines differed from company to company, and even procedures in the regional offices of some national accounting firms depended on local interpretation. Buyers and sellers of land and improved property were free to report the profit from almost any transaction that was mutually acceptable to both parties.

The structuring of real estate sales and exchanges was at its creative high in the late 1960s when the Internal Revenue Service questioned the practice of buyers prepaying interest for as long as five years and acquiring property with little or no payment against the principal. This had become the common practice of individuals in high-income brackets and privately held companies and partnerships who took full advantage of the tax write-off permitted by the federal government.

The Securities and Exchange Commission (SEC) then began to investigate the windfall profits reported by public companies involved in real estate sales, especially retail-lots sales. SEC's thorough analysis of the balance sheets of these companies revealed that many of them were cash poor and in a serious liquidity position but still continued to report huge profits. The Commission considered this misleading to investors.

In 1973 the American Institute of Certified Public Accountants (AICPA) issued two important industry accounting guides, the first nationally accepted, authoritative literature that established rules for all accounting firms to apply uniformly to both private and public entities. The two AICPA guides—*Accounting for Profit Recognition on Sales of Real Estate* and *Accounting for Retail Land Sales*—detail when a sale is a sale for profit recognition and the related accounting practices that should be adhered to in financial reporting. (Copies of both publications can be obtained for a nominal charge from the American Institute of Certified Public Accountants; 1211 Avenue of the Americas; New York, N.Y. 10036.)

The impact of the AICPA publications on public companies was significant, and private companies and individuals were also materially affected. The IRS had already disallowed the long-term prepayment of interest and had reduced the interest deductible for tax purposes to one year. Stringent government legislation enacted on federal and state levels affected retail land sales. Now the AICPA establishes minimum down payment requirements of cash or "hard dollars" before a company can recognize its profit on a real estate transaction.

Many public companies were required to restate their earnings, and huge profits suddenly became huge losses. Private businesses and individuals quickly realized that if they did not comply with the new AICPA guidelines their accountants might express adverse opinions about the financial statements involved. When interpreted by a lender, such statements could drastically limit the financial capabilities and leverage of net worth of the business in question.

To further compound matters, the IRS took the position of taxing *possible* profits, and the accounting profession was conservative in limiting or eliminating reportable profits if *any doubt* existed as to the collectibility of the receivable. This meant that a transaction might not be recorded as profitable on a financial statement, but could still be considered profitable by the IRS for tax purposes.

20 AND 25% PROPERTY

The terms "Exhibit A" and the "115% test" have become new words in the real estate industry's vocabulary. Other than retail-lot sales, for a sale to be considered reportable and profitable, the down payment must meet one of these two accounting criteria. The rules apply universally to large and small public and private companies, as well as to individuals.

Since established lending institutions ordinarily loan 50–95% of the value of the real estate, Kenneth Leventhal & Company has prepared a table that indicates the amount of down payment required as a percentage of sales value for a sale that meets all other guidelines to be considered for profit recognition. This compilation includes both Exhibit A and the 115% test (see pages 128–129).

The minimum down payment required to recognize profit on a sale of real estate should be the amount derived from Exhibit A *or* the amount by which the sales value of the property exceeds 115% of the amount of the loan or commitment by the primary lender, *whichever is greater.* Usually, a down payment that is equal to 60% of the difference between a lender's appraised value of the property and a maximum first lien loan is also equal to or greater than the difference between the sales value and 115% of the primary loan.

Exhibit A is a schedule of minimum down payments established by the AICPA for various types of real estate property to determine whether or not a buyer's initial investment is sufficient to recognize revenue and profit at the time of sale. Exhibit A outlines real property, ranging from a low of 5% for single-family residential property, which is the primary residence of the buyer, to 25% for land held for commercial, industrial, or residential development after two years.

The accounting profession classifies undeveloped land based on when it is to be used: 25% property is land held for development after a two-year period, whereas 20% property is land on which development is to begin within two years of the sale.

Kenneth Leventhal & Company warns that special caution should be exercised in situations in which there are high loan-to-value ratios and the seller remains primarily or secondarily liable on the primary debt: 80% or more for 25% property, and 90% or more of loan-to-value ratio for 20% property.

Accountants use both tests to determine if the buyer's initial investment is large enough that he does not risk losing the property by default. This gives the seller reasonable assurance that he will be able to collect his sales price.

The down payment must consist of cash or a cashlike equivalent, such as irrevocable letters of credit. Marketable securities, for example, may not be used in lieu of cash, even if the stock is considered blue chip or is a AAA+ municipal or corporate bond.

Down Payment Required as a Percentage of Sales Value

Loan/Value Ratio	25% Property (Land held for commercial, industrial, or residential development after 2 years.)	20% Property (Land held for commercial, industrial, or residential development to commence within 2 years after sale.)
50%	25%	25%*
51%	25%	25%*
52%	25%	25%*
53%	25%	25%*
54%	25%	25%*
55%	25%	25%*
56%	25%	25%*
57%	25%	25%*
58%	25%	25%*
59%	25%	25%*
60%	25%	25%*
61%	25%	25%*
62%	25%	25%*
63%	25%	25%*
64%	25%	25%*
65%	25%	25%*
66%	25%	24%
67%	25%	23%
68%	25%	21.75%
69%	25%	20.5%
70%	25%	20%
71%	25%	20%
72%	25%	20%
73%	25%	20%
74%	25%	20%
75%	25%	20%
76%	24%#	20%
77%	23%#	20%
78%	22%#	20%
79%	21%#	20%
80%	20%#	20%
81%	19%#	19%#
82%	18%#	18%#
83%	17%#	17%#
84%	16%#	16%#
85%	15%#	15%#
86%	14%#	14%#
87%	13%#	13%#

Down Payment Required as a Percentage of Sales Value (Continued)

Loan/Value Ratio	25% Property (Land held for commercial, industrial, or residential development after 2 years.)	20% Property (Land held for commercial, industrial, or residential development to commence within 2 years after sale.)
88%	12%#	12%#
89%	11%#	11%#
90%	10%#	10%#
91%	9%#	9%#
92%	8%#	8%#
93%	7%#	7%#
94%	6%#	6%#
95%	5%#	5%#

Legend: 00% —Down payment from Exhibit A test governs.

00%*—Down payment from 115% test governs; however, the maximum required down payment is 25%.

00%#—Down payment from Exhibit A test governs; however, the maximum required down payment is cash-to-loan ratio. Caution should be exercised in situations in which there are high loan/value ratios and the seller remains primarily or secondarily liable on the primary debt.

NOTE: Down payment percentages have been rounded to the nearest .25%.

For practical reasons, however, the individual or the small, private company does have somewhat of a reporting advantage over his public counterparts or larger private companies. How a transaction is reported may not really be that important.

CONTINUED BUYER COMMITMENT

To recognize revenue and profit on the sale of any real property, the buyer must meet not only the down payment requirement but his annual amortization payment. "For example, a buyer who has met the down payment tests but who is scheduled to make no payments except for interest during the next four years, and who then pays off the full amount in the fifth year, would not meet this rule," says Kurt Alexander.

On a first mortgage the buyer must make annual payments until the amount paid equals the total indebtedness, including interest on the unpaid balance, over the term of the mortgage. The buyer must also amortize any second trust deed over a period of time by an amount that is no more than the amount customarily extended on the first mortgage. This means that there can be no "sleeping seconds," in which the buyer pays only interest for a number of years and then has a balloon payment. A profit may be recognized if the buyer pays interest only on the second mortgage, but at a reduced rate because the payments will be discounted as if they represent combined interest and principal payments.

CONTINUED INVOLVEMENT OF THE SELLER

If the seller remains involved with the property after it is sold, he may have to defer reporting all or some of his profit. This can happen if the seller is granted an option to repurchase, for example. Even if the seller receives 100% cash for the purchase, it cannot be recorded if he has any option to repurchase the property, regardless of the time or duration of the option. Further continuing involvement can be in the form of a sale leaseback or an obligation to place improvements on the property.

Of particular interest to private developers and individual landholders, profit cannot be reported when the seller participates as a general partner, either directly or indirectly, and holds large receivables (15% of the maximum first lien) for which sole repayment is from the property.

A company participating in a project may be permitted to sell its portion of the land if no control exists and if its involvement in the project is limited to a proportionate share of profits and losses. When the owners hold disproportionate shares and buyer preference exists, profits should be recognized by other methods.

LEASES, LEASE OPTIONS, AND SUBORDINATION

If the property is leased over a period of time and reverts back to the seller when the contract terminates, no sale is recorded but income is recognizable over the period of the lease.

A lease option is not a sale, but income derived during the period of the lease is recognized as income. The same accounting rules apply at the time of sale, but some portion of the income during the period of the lease option may be credited to the down payment.

The sale of land subject to future subordination of the seller's receivable is subject to special reporting rules. When the seller guarantees return of the buyer's investment or is granted a repurchase option, buyer "puts," or long-term guarantees, the income must be treated as a financing, leasing, or profit-sharing arrangement.

OTHER METHODS OF ACCOUNTING FOR PROFIT

During economic down cycles a public company may sell land where a 25% down payment is required, but because of prevailing conditions the company may accept 15% down and let the buyer continue to make the payments. Clearly, the initial down payment is less than Exhibit A or the 115% test. The seller cannot report the sale at the time of closing, but one of the following accounting methods will apply: deposit accounting, the installment method, or cost recovery.

Deposit Accounting.   This method postpones recognizing a sale until it can be determined that the sale has occurred for accounting purposes. The seller records no receivable, and continues to show the property as an asset and the deposit as a liability; the status of the property is disclosed on the financial statements.

Installment Method.   This method is used to report profits as principal payments are received. Any portion of the payment that is credited to interest is not credited against the down payment. A certain segment of each payment is considered recovery of the seller's cost and a certain segment is recognized as income, but recognition extends over the full life of the contract as payments are received.

Cost Recovery.   This method is employed when there is a substantial uncertainty that all or even a portion of the cost can be recovered if the buyer defaults. Accountants must face so many uncertainties in collecting receivables that they would hesitate to predict something unforseeable, such as a zoning rollback, an environmental moratorium, or some other problem. If there is an irrevocable transaction, here is what might happen:

Sales price	$1,000,000
Cost of property	300,000
Down payment	200,000

This down payment meets Exhibit A for 20% property with a loan/value ratio of 70–80%, or Exhibit A for 25% property with an 80% loan commitment. The down payment is initially applied to the recovery of cost. If a subsequent payment of $150,000 were made, the first $100,000 would fully absorb the balance of the cost on the books. The remaining $50,000 and any additional amount credited to principal would then qualify and be recognized as full income.

RETAIL LAND SALES

Prior to the issuance of the AICPA guide *Accounting for Retail Land Sales*, most lot-sale companies used the accrual method of accounting to record data. There were no stringent down payment requirements. The sale was recorded in full (the expense of the land, selling expenses, and estimated charge for amenities and improvements that might not be constructed for several years), a reserve for cancellation was deducted from the sale, and the balance was recorded as profit.

Because of their accounting methods, many of these companies reflected tremendous profits on their financial statements before they had really received a good commitment from the buyer, before they had demonstrated an ability to construct improvements at the projected cost, and before the earnings process had actually been completed.

Because down payments were very low, a buyer who had probably bought the lot sight unseen could walk away from his commitment, leaving the seller with no enforceable recourse.

The new AICPA guidelines established criteria for both the buyer and the seller. A sale can now only be recorded when the buyer has made the down payment and each regular installment payment required until the period of cancellation with refund has expired, when payments on principal and interest equal or exceed 10% of the contract sales price, and when the selling company has demonstrated its financial capability to provide the improvements and facilities it has promised. Until such conditions are met, monies collected should be recorded as deposits.

The new AICPA rules require a company to recognize its profits on retail land sales either by the accrual or the installment method.

THE ACCRUAL METHOD

The accrual method of accounting allows a company to record the portion of its profit that is related to land sale and to defer recording its profit for work to be constructed and to recognize this profit as improvements are completed.

The AICPA states that the accrual method should be applied only when contract collections are reasonably assured and when the following additional conditions are met: that the property be in a useful state for residential or recreational purposes at the end of the normal payment period; that there is evidence the improvements have progressed beyond the preliminary stage and are being developed as promised by the seller; that the contract receivable is not subject to subordination to new loans on the property, except in certain cases; and that the company's collection experience allows it to estimate that 90% of the contracts in force six months after sales are recorded will be collected.

The AICPA rules do permit a substitution to be made in the last condition, based on the amount of the buyer's investment. The greater the buyer's investment in the property, the less likely he will be to risk contract default and to forfeit his down payment and any money he has paid on the contract.

Based on retail sales experience in the land industry, the accounting profession has established a table to determine when receivables should be considered uncollectable if regular payments due are unpaid for the following delinquency periods:

Percent of Contract Price Paid	Delinquency Period
Less than 25%	90 days
25%, but less than 50%	120 days
50% and over	150 days

Kenneth Leventhal & Company warns that it is difficult to estimate, evaluate, and predict certain conditions using the accrual method. For example, can the same rule of thumb be applied to collectable receivables during the economic conditions the nation faced in 1974 and 1975? What happens if the developer is financially able to provide improvements according to plan, but his progress is interrupted by environmental or ecological considerations that were not anticipated when the sale was made?

If a company cannot meet the AICPA standards established for the accrual method of accounting, it must use the installment method to recognize its profits. When a company is qualified to use the accrual method, it is preferred by the AICPA.

THE INSTALLMENT METHOD

The installment method results in less profit recognition at the time a sale is made, because the profit is deferred over the term of the contract. The primary reason many companies use the installment method is that it is more difficult to predict the collection of receivables using the accrual method.

Using the installment method, the entire contract price applicable to the installment sale, with no reduction for cancellations or discounts, is included as gross revenue on the company's income statements during the year the sale is recorded. The cost of sales, including provisions for all amenities and improvements, selling, and general and administrative expenses, is charged against the company's recognized income during the same period. The resultant gross profit is then be reduced by profits that are to be deferred to a future period pursuant to the installment calculation.

Interest on the receivables is reported as income when it is received. Cancellations are recorded by removing the unpaid receivables from the accounts, by restoring recoverable costs to land and improvements, by reducing the liability for future improvements applicable to the contract, and by decreasing the applicable unamortized deferred profits.

Income can be recognized on the company's financial statements using both the installment and the accrual methods of accounting. A company can change from the installment to the accrual method when sufficient cash has been collected to qualify the sale for accrual accounting.

TAXES AND PROFITS

The new AICPA guidelines have created a set of rules that are universally operable and applicable. However, these guidelines have also created paradoxical situations in which transactions are reportable for tax purposes but are not reportable for accounting purposes.

A seller must be careful not to put himself in the position of having to recognize taxable income but having no income that he can report on his financial statements. Each transaction must be analyzed intelligently at the time of sale, both from a tax point of view and an accounting point of view. Individuals and private companies who are forced to report to lenders should be extremely sensitive not to create taxable income and incur tax liabilities ahead of statement income.

Kurt Alexander offers the following example. Company A buys a parcel of land for $85,000, completes certain engineering work at a cost of $15,000, and then sells the property to Company B for $200,000 cash. The economic profit from the sale of this parcel is:

Sales price		$200,000
Cost of sales		
Land	$85,000	
Engineering	15,000	100,000
Gross profit		100,000
Tax liability on profit		50,000
Net economic profit		$ 50,000

If the seller does not continue to be involved in the property and if other prerequisites are met, the economic profit shown above is company A's financial profit.

However, suppose Company A has agreed to complete work on the site development as a continuing involvement. If the development work costs $300,000, the cost to the developer based on firm contracts is $270,000. This contract added to the land sale indicates that the seller remains involved with the property after the sale, and under the new AICPA rules an allocation of total income based on costs incurred to total estimated costs is required.

Kurt Alexander illustrates the way financial income is calculated:

Total income:

	Sale of Land	Site Development	Total
Income	$ 200,000	$ 300,000	$ 500,000
Costs	100,000	270,000	370,000
Gross profit	$ 100,000	$ 30,000	$ 130,000

Income reportable after the disposition of the land:

$$\frac{\text{Cost of land}}{\text{Cost of land} + \text{Cost of site development}} \times \text{Total gross profit}$$
$$= \text{Reportable gross profit}$$

$$\frac{\$100,000}{\$100,000 + \$270,000} \times \$130,000 = \$35,126$$

The reportable gross profit of $35,126 results in a tax of $17,563 on the company's financial statements. Assuming a 50% tax bracket, this leaves a net profit contribution of $17,563. Although the developer's economic net worth has increased $50,000 after paying income taxes of $50,000, the company's financial statements reflect a net profit of only $17,563 because of the developer's continuing involvement with the property after the sale.

ECONOMICS OR EARNINGS?

Public companies are pressured by shareholders and by Wall Street to continually report earnings rather than deferred profits. The approved AICPA guidelines must be followed in recognizing and reporting profits. However, Kenneth Leventhal & Company, Certified Public Accountants, advises businessmen and companies, even if public, that the new accounting principles should not dictate economic decisions.

When real estate companies were the "glamour" stocks of Wall Street and commanded high price–earnings multiples, they were encouraged to "manage" earnings so that growth could be shown each quarter and each year. When the stock market started its downward slide in 1973, increased earnings did not help to build investor confidence or to move the price of the stock, even at low price–earnings multiples. Some public companies took the position that they could make more money in the long run by selling land that might not conform to the AICPA guidelines but that was more economical. Profits on sales could not be reported when the transactions occurred unless minimum down payments were made, but profits would be recorded eventually if the sales were bona fide.

The problem can be illustrated this way: A seller of land has two offers:

Buyer A	$ 1,500,000, with 10% down
Buyer B	1,000,000, with 25% down

The decision should be based on economics and not necessarily on compliance with accounting rules, unless it is essential that the seller report earnings and he is in need of the additional $100,000 cash. The seller would receive $150,000 from Buyer A and $250,000 from Buyer B. Naturally, all conditions of the sales contract would have to be carefully examined.

CHAPTER XIV

GOVERNMENT REGULATION

Depending on how a sale is structured, how much land is being sold, and how and to whom it is being sold, the seller should obtain legal counsel and advice regarding government regulation of the sale.

Today there is a virtual proliferation of layer on layer of government regulation regarding land sales and transactions. Much of it is for the good and protection of the consumer, but much of it adds to the frustration of real estate agents, particularly when one agency does not recognize the approval of another or when totally different sets of forms requesting virtually the same information must be prepared and filed.

A seller must be concerned with state and federal regulations as well as with the requirements of government agencies that have become involved in land utilization. Any question regarding an interstate sale of land should be directed to the Office of Interstate Land Sales Registration. Each state also maintains an agency that requires prior approval of an interstate or a intrastate sale.

Moreover, it is important to be knowledgeable about recent actions of the Federal Trade Commission (FTC) and the Environmental Protection Agency (EPA).

For example, the FTC has actively been filing complaints against many large companies involved in interstate land sales. In one case the FTC proposed that the seller be required to warn buyers with information that included the following statement:

You should consider the purchase of any of our land to be very risky. Few if any purchasers of land from . . . , or its subsidiaries, have been able to resell such land at a profit. Purchasers usually have been unable to resell the land at all.

The EPA is one agency that has compounded problems for the real estate industry. State and local governments establish their own laws regarding air, water, and noise pollution. For some projects, prior approval must be obtained not only from local jurisdictions but from the EPA as well. In some instances approval can be obtained from a state or local government but not from the EPA, and vice versa. This essentially renders the land unbuildable or undevelopable as a result of bureaucratic red tape or interagency jealousy.

The biggest problems for the real estate professional occur in ambiguous, unclear, or grey areas, where interpretation and definition are at the discretion of a regional office of a federal agency. All too often a federal agency or department does not clearly define its intent, and when a local bureaucrat, who does not fully understand the development process must make a decision, the decision is to make no decision at all, which creates an impasse.

OILSR

The Office of Interstate Land Sales Registration (OILSR) is part of the U.S. Department of Housing and Urban Development. It was established by the Interstate Land Sales Full Disclosure Act as Title XIV of the Housing and Urban Development Act of 1968, which became effective April 28, 1969. The Act was patterned after the Securities Act of 1933.

The Housing and Urban Development Act applies to the sale of vacant lots in subdivisions that are promoted by "any means or instruments of transportation or communication in interstate commerce, or of the mails" and that contain 50 or more lots. Certain statutory exemptions include:

• The sale of a lot with a building thereon or under contract that obligates the seller to erect a building thereon within two years from the date of the lot sale.
• Subdivisions in which all lots are five acres or larger in size, in addition to other statutory and regulatory exemptions.

Rules, regulations, and guidelines are always being changed, so it is important to check with the OILSR before undertaking any program. Registrations filed with OILSR are accepted by 17 states as the equivalent of their registration requirements, and the agency has been working with other states to secure a uniform registration procedure.

Several OILSR publications are available. Recommended are:

- Statute 15 USC 1701-1720
- Regulations 24 CFR 1700, 1710, 1715, and 1720
- HUD Handbook 1166.1 Organization of the Office of Interstate Land Sales Registration.
- Consumer publications:
  "Get the Facts Before Buying Land" HUD 183-1-(4)
  "Buying Lots from Developers" HUD 357-1-(4)

Questions concerning OILSR rules, regulations, future amendments, and program information can be addressed to:

> Office of Interstate Land Sales Registration
> U.S. Department of Housing and Urban Development
> 451 Seventh Street, S.W.
> Washington, D.C. 20410
> (202) 755-5860

STATE REGULATION

Different government agencies are responsible for administering and enforcing real estate regulations in various states. Because laws differ, it is important to obtain information from the responsible agency.

A seller should determine the answers to a number of questions, including:

- Is registration required for a sale or offering of subdivided land located within the state? Outside the state?
- What number of lots comprises the definition of a subdivision?
- Are on-site inspections required before a subdivision can be granted an effective registration?
- Must annual reports be filed?
- Are buyers afforded any period of time to rescind the sale? If so, what is the duration of the recision period?
- What advertising and promotional materials, plans, or programs must be approved or reviewed prior to their use?
- Does the state accept the developer's effective filing with the OILSR as a substitute for state filing?
- Can materials containing information about the sales offering be mailed into the state from outside the state?

- Can advertising appear in national or regional magazines without registration in the state?
- Can prospective buyers be telephoned from outside the state?
- Are any special promotions or incentives prohibited?

The American Land Development Association has published a complete report of state regulations that answers many of these questions. The publication, *The Digest of State Land Sales Regulations,* lists the following sources of information about land sales in each state, as well as in Canada and Mexico:

Alabama

Alabama Real Estate Commission
562 State Office Building
Montgomery, AL 36104
(205) 269-6242

Supervisor
License Tax Division
Department of Revenue
Montgomery, AL 36102
(205) 832-6740

Alaska

Director
Division of Banking, Securities, Small Loans, and Corporations
Department of Commerce
Pouch D
Juneau, AK 99801

Arizona

Arizona Real Estate Department
1645 West Jefferson
Phoenix, AZ 85007
(602) 271-4347

Arkansas

Arkansas Real Estate Commission
1311 West Second Street
P.O. Box 3173
Little Rock, AR 72201
(501) 371-1247

California
Department of Real Estate
Suite 1400
714 P Street
Sacramento, CA 95814
(916) 445-3996

Colorado
Colorado Real Estate Commission
110 State Services Building
1525 Sherman Street
Denver, CO 80203
(303) 892-2633

Connecticut
Connecticut Real Estate Commission
90 Washington Street
Hartford, CT 06115
(203) 566-5130

Delaware
Delaware Real Estate Commission
State House Annex
Dover, DE 19901
(302) 678-4186

District of Columbia
Government of the District of Columbia
Room 107
614 H Street, N.W.
Washington, D.C. 20001

Florida
State of Florida
Department of Business Regulation
Division of Florida Land Sales
P.O. Box 4448
Tampa, FL 33677
(813) 272-3845

Georgia
Office of the Secretary of State
State Capital
Atlanta, GA 30334

Georgia State Securities Commission
State Capital
Atlanta, GA 30334

Hawaii

State of Hawaii
Professional and Vocational Licensing Division
Department of Regulatory Agencies
P.O. Box 3469

Land Use Commission
Department of Agriculture
State of Hawaii
250 S. King Street
Honolulu, HW 96813
(808) 548-4611

Idaho

Idaho State Real Estate Commission
633 North Fourth Street
Boise, ID 83720
(208) 384-3285

Illinois

Assistant Real Estate Commissioner
Land Sales Section
Department of Registration and Education
Room 1700
55 East Jackson Blvd.
Chicago, IL 60604
(312) 341-9810; extension 233

Indiana

Indiana Real Estate Commission
1022 State Office Building
100 North Senate Avenue
Indianapolis, IN 46204
(317) 633-5386

Iowa

Iowa Real Estate Commission
Executive Hills
1223 East Court
Des Moines, IA 50319
(515) 281-3183

Assistant Attorney General
Consumer Protection Division
Iowa Department of Justice
1209 East Court
Executive Hills West
Des Moines, IA 50319
(515) 281-5926

Kansas
Division of Land Registration
Securities Commission
State Office Building
Topeka, KN 66612
(913) 296-3307

Kentucky
Kentucky Real Estate Commission
100 East Liberty Street
Louisville, KY 40202
(502) 583-2771

Louisiana
Department of Occupational Standards
Real Estate Commission
P.O. Box 44095
Capital Station
Baton Rouge, LA 70804
(504) 389-5253

Maine
State of Maine
Environmental Improvement Commission
Augusta, ME 04330

Department of Banks and Banking
Securities Division
State Office Annex
Capital Shopping Center
Augusta, ME 04330
(207) 289-2261

Maryland
Maryland Real Estate Commission
One Calvert Street
Baltimore, MD 21201
(301) 383-2130

Department of State Planning
1103 State Office Building
Baltimore, MD 21201

Massachusetts
Division of Registration
Board of Registration of Real Estate
100 Cambridge Street
Boston, MA 02202
(617) 727-3055

Michigan
Director
Land Sales Division
Department of Licensing and Regulation
1008 South Washington Avenue
Lansing, MI 48926
(517) 373-7360

Minnesota
Commissioner of Securities
Securities Division
500 Metro Square Building
St. Paul, MN 55101
(612) 296-6848

Mississippi
Mississippi Real Estate Commission
Busby Building
754 North President Street
Jackson, MS 39202
(601) 354-7093

Missouri
Commissioner of Securities
Office of the Secretary of State
Capital Building
Jefferson City, MO 65101
(314) 751-4136

Missouri Real Estate Commission
3523 North Ten Mile Drive
Jefferson City, MO 65101
(314) 751-2334

Chief Counsel
Consumer Protection Division
Attorney General of Missouri
Supreme Court Building
Jefferson City, MO 65101
(314) 751-3555

Montana
Administrator
Montana Board of Real Estate
LaLonde Building
42   North Main Street
Helena, MT 59601
(406) 449-2961

Nebraska
Nebraska Real Estate Commission
P.O. Box 94667
State Capital Building
Lincoln, NB 68509
(402) 471-2004

Nevada
Real Estate Division
Department of Commerce
Suite 200
111 West Telegraph Street
Carson City, NV 89701
(702) 882-7509

New Hampshire
Land Sales Division
State of New Hampshire
State House Annex
Concord, NH 03301
(603) 271-3641

New Jersey
Director
New Jersey Real Estate Commission
201 East State Street
Trenton, NJ 08625
(609) 292-7053

New Mexico
    Land Fraud Division
    Office of the Attorney General
    P.O. Box 2246
    Santa Fe, NM 87501
    (505) 827-2844

New York
    Office of the Secretary of State
    Department of State
    270 Broadway
    New York, NY 10007
    (212) 488-3158

North Carolina
    North Carolina Real Estate Licensing Board
    P.O. Box 266
    Raleigh, NC 27602
    (919) 833-2771

    Department of Justice
    Office of Attorney General
    State Capital
    Raleigh, NC 27602
    (919) 829-3377

North Dakota
    North Dakota Real Estate Commission
    410 East Thayer Avenue
    P.O. Box 727
    Bismark, ND 58501
    (701) 224-2749

Ohio
    Securities Division
    Department of Commerce
    180 East Broad Street
    Columbus, OH 43215
    (614) 466-3440

Oklahoma
    Oklahoma Real Estate Commission
    Suite 100
    4040 Lincoln Blvd.
    Oklahoma City, OK 73105
    (405) 521-3387

Oregon
    Supervisor
    Subdivision Section
    Real Estate Division
    Department of Commerce
    Salem, OR 97310
    (503) 378-8422

Pennsylvania
    Commissioner of Professional and Occupational Affairs
    279 Boas Street
    Harrisburg, PA 17120

    Assistant Attorney General for Consumer Practices
    Department of Justice
    2-4 North Market Square
    Harrisburg, PA 17101
    (717) 787-2338

    Pennsylvania Real Estate Commission
    P.O. Box 2649
    Harrisburg, PA 17120

Rhode Island
    Director of Business Regulation
    Real Estate Division
    169 Weybosset Street
    Providence, RI 02903
    (401) 227-2255

South Carolina
    Commissioner
    South Carolina Real Estate Commission
    900 Elmwood Avenue
    Columbia, SC 29201
    (803) 758-3981

South Dakota
    South Dakota Real Estate Commission
    319 South Coteau
    P.O. Box 638
    Pierre, SD 57501
    (605) 224-3600

Tennessee

Department of Insurance
Division of Securities
204 State Office Building
Nashville, TN 37219
(615) 741-2947, or 741-3186

Real Estate Commission
Capital Hill Building
Nashville, TN 37219

Texas

Texas Real Estate Commission
P.O. Box 12188
Capital Station
Austin, TX 78711
(512) 475-4247

State Securities Board
P.O. Box 13167
Capitol Station
Austin, TX 78711
(512) 475-4561

Assistant Attorney General
Antitrust and Consumer Protection Division
Supreme Court Building
Austin, TX 78711
(512) 475-3288

Utah

Director
Department of Business Regulation
Real Estate Division
330 East Fourth South Street
Salt Lake City, UT 84111
(801) 328-5661

Vermont

Securities Division
Department of Banking and Insurance
Montpelier, VT 05602
(802) 828-3301

Real Estate Commission
7 East State Street
Montpelier, VT 05602
(802) 828-3228

Virginia
Virginia Real Estate Commission
P.O. Box 1-X
Richmond, VA 23202
(804) 770-7285

Washington
Real Estate Division
Land Development Registration and Administration
P.O. Box 247
Olympia, WA 98504
(206) 753-6909

West Virginia
Deputy Securities Commissioner
State Auditor's Office
Charleston, WV 25305
(304) 348-2257

Real Estate Commission
Building 3, Room 402
State Capital
Charleston, WV 25305

Wisconsin
Department of Regulation and Licensing
Real Estate Examining Board
819 North Sixth Street
Milwaukee, WI 53203
(414) 224-4491

Wyoming
Commissioner
Wyoming Real Estate Commission
2219 Carey Avenue
Cheyenne, WY 82002
(307) 777-7011

CANADA

Alberta
Deputy Superintendent
Office of the Superintendent of Insurance and Real Estate
Petroleum Plaza South, 9th floor
9915 108th Street
Edmonton, Alberta T5K 2H7
(403) 427-2244

British Columbia
Real Estate Council of British Columbia
Suite 608
626 West Pender Street
Vancouver, B.C. V6B 1V9
(604) 683-9664

Manitoba
Registrar
The Real Estate Brokers Act
Room 203
379 Broadway Avenue
Winnipeg, Manitoba R3C OT9
(204) 942-0761

Ontario
Foreign Lands Officer
The Real Estate and Business Brokers Act
Ministry of Consumer and Commercial Relations
555 Yonge Street
Toronto, Ontario M4Y 1Y7
(416) 965-2504

Quebec
Superintendent
Real Estate Brokerage Branch
Department of Consumers, Cooperatives, and Financial
    Institutions
Hotel du Gouvernement
Quebec, Quebec
(418) 643-4597

Saskatchewan
Superintendent of Insurance
Province of Saskatchewan

Room 308
1919 Rose Street
Regina, Saskatchewan S4P 3P1
(306) 527-0101

MEXICO

Secretariat of Foreign Relations
Mexico, D. F., Mexico

CHAPTER XV

FOREIGN INVESTMENT OPPORTUNITIES

Investment in land in a foreign country can be rewarding, but it can also present many risks that do not confront investors in the United States. However, for a primary investor-developer, who is aware of the special disciplines necessary to assure a profitable return, the financial rewards can be very great.

There are three basic ways to invest in foreign land, and each method can be a combination of variously structured entities.

The *developer* or *general partner* is the corporation, partnership or individual responsible for packaging the project, providing the management, and overseeing the invested funds. The developer may play the role of promoter or syndicator in raising investment capital, or he may actually be responsible for planning, constructing, and developing the project.

The *limited partner-investor* is a passive investor seeking a high return on capital. Based on the structure of participation in the project and on legal and financial counsel opportunities may be found to shelter some or all of the return or to defer reporting profits and gains.

The *individual user* invests in land as a site for a second or retirement home. The profit opportunities in buying an interest in a lot or parcel of land that is part of a subdivision in a foreign country are minimal compared to being a major or sale investor in foreign land.

Many lots can be purchased on an installment plan, and some owners have resold their land at a profit. But most individual-user investors consider the reward to be the use of the site, rather than its value appreciation.

MEXICAN REQUIREMENTS FOR FOREIGNERS

Mexico has established specific constitutional laws and regulations stating how land can be acquired. Only Mexicans by birth or naturalization or Mexican corporations have the right to direct ownership of Mexican land.

No foreigner or foreign entity may directly own any land or water within a strip 100 kilometers wide along the borders or 50 kilometers wide along the coastline. Further, no foreign individual or entity may even be a partner in a Mexican corporation that can acquire such ownership within these restricted zones.

However, the Mexican government may grant the same rights to aliens that are accorded Mexican citizens if alien individuals or entities agree before the Ministry of Foreign Relations to be considered Mexican regarding property ownership and not to invoke the protection of their governments in property matters. Violators of this agreement must forfeit the acquired property to the Mexican government.

If a foreigner inherits rights that are denied aliens by Mexican law, the Ministry of Foreign Relations grants permission for the adjudication and registration of the respective deed. If that foreigner, by virtue of a preexisting right acquired in good faith, should then have to assume some right prohibited by Mexican law, the government can grant permission for such adjudication. In both cases a permit is conditionally granted that enables the foreigner to transfer his rights to a person who is legally capable of holding them within five years of the death of the testator or the adjudication.

The only foreigners who can acquire real estate or real rights after obtaining a permit from the Ministry of the Interior are political refugees and students, in exceptional cases, and immigrants, if the acquisition does not conflict with their migratory status. A permit is never issued to nonimmigrants, such as tourists, persons in transit, and visitors.

MEXICAN INVESTMENT THROUGH TRUSTS

A foreign individual or corporation can hold personal rights to real estate in Mexico, including the prohibited coastal and border zones, through a real estate trust. According to the Banco de Comercio, S.A., the foreign individual or entity is the beneficiary of the land trust and holds a personal right to use, lease, sell, modify, or live on the property. This right is limited to 30 years, the legal duration of the trust, and real property title is held in a deed of trust by the trustee. Mexican law specifies that only authorized institutions may act as trustee and exercise the trustee's responsibilities, and that the beneficiary's personal property rights must be exercised through a bank. At the end of 30 years (sooner, if the trust is terminated for any reason), the property is sold to a qualified buyer, and the proceeds revert to the beneficiary or to his legal heirs.

The legal requirements of the trust and the procedures for establishing it are determined by the nature of the trust. The two most common trusts permit the construction or purchase of a single private home on land of not more than 2000 square meters and the development or purchase of resort or industrial facilities.

The parties to a Mexican real estate trust are:

• *Trustor:* A Mexican corporation with no foreign participants, or a citizen who is the original owner of the real estate and who places the property in trust.

• *Trustee:* The banking institution that holds the trust over the land for the beneficiary.

• *Beneficiary:* Normally the promoter who acquires beneficial rights to develop the property and then sells its beneficial interest to other parties. The final beneficiary is the party who buys beneficiary rights from the promoter or other final beneficiaries. The final beneficiary is almost always a foreigner, because Mexicans ordinarily buy direct ownership.

Authorization for a trust is generally granted only if foreign promoters form a joint venture with a Mexican individual or corporation; in such cases the foreign interest is usually limited to 49% of the entity's stock. Three common types of trusts are used in the development of large projects. The structure of the trust depends on whether the project is divisible and provides a method to convey beneficial rights to third parties:

• *Nondivisable trust:* When a project is nondivisible (is to be main-

tained as a single, intact unit), such as hotels and industrial plants, this
type of trust reflects the expected unity of the project and ownership.

• *Spinning or development trust:* When a large project is undertaken
that includes several units of development and that may be phased over
time and handled by different promoters, an initial trust is established
over the entire project. This is essentially a system of trusts generated
from one original trust. As elements of the project are used for the
development of hotels, home subdivisions, condominiums, or clubs, the
original beneficiaries instruct the trustee to establish a new trust covering only this phase, and the developers of the new and separate units
become first beneficiaries of these smaller trusts.

• *Master trust:* When subdivision is anticipated at the outset, a master
trust conveys interest from the first beneficiary to a direct contact with
the final beneficiary, such as the purchaser of a unit in a condominium.
Two advantages of the master trust are the relative ease with which
authorization for its establishment can be obtained and with which the
cession of beneficiary rights to third parties can be made.

ENTERING THE MEXICAN MARKET

Pancho Hunt of the Lincoln Property Company, Santa Monica,
California, and Compañia Mexicana de Fomento Urbanistico,
Guadalajara, Jalisco, Mexico, warns that it is difficult to get into the
real estate business in Mexico. "There are a number of risks involved,
but it is very possible the total gain could be considerably higher than
in the United States, but only in proportion to the risk. Anyone investing in Mexico should get two to three times the return they would
expect in the United States to compensate for the additional risk.

"The first and most important step to take is to seek out a very well
recommended lawyer and accountant. Remember, you are dealing with
a foreign country, foreign laws, and many things don't mesh together
the way one might ordinarily be accustomed to doing business. Do not
make any commitment until you have had many long discussions with
professional counselors," he advises.

Hunt believes the best way U.S. developers or investor groups can
protect themselves in Mexico is to operate on a joint-venture basis with
the landowner, so that if the project cannot be completed for any
reason, only the front-end cost is risked and not the land itself.

Hunt's companies have been involved in joint ventures in Puerto
Vallarta and Guadalajara with a Mexican landowner on a 51-49%
basis. The Mexican partner contributes the land at an agreed-on value,

which is generally less than the appraised market value. The U.S. developer contributes all the necessary costs from architectural and planning fees to management, construction, supervision, and overhead. Hunt seeks projects that can be completed within two or three years.

"When the project is sold, the construction and development costs are paid off first. Then there is a distribution of the profits based on a preagreed percentage basis, which can vary from deal to deal. An American investor should look to an equal distribution of the participation in the venture, or 49%."

According to Hunt, there are very few competent, professional real estate developers in Mexico compared to the United States. "Because of this, there are excellent joint-venture opportunities for American companies that have a proven record of performance," Hunt states.

Major development problems in Mexico include the absence of title documentation, title insurance, and escrows. The better long-term, conventional financing is a 75% loan commitment for a term of 15 years, which Hunt arranged for one project through the real estate trust of a U.S. bank.

Legal services are vitally important in determining ownership of land. "Mexico has a communal farming system called a Ejido, and the Ejidatarios who live on these farms in principle own the land and have rights of ownership, but they cannot sell it. They have the rights as long as they live on the land, but once they die title cannot be transferred, but the ownership rights probably will be assumed by heirs. It may be virtually impossible to trace back through several generations whether or not the land someone may wish to sell or transfer title to is or is not Ejido land," says Hunt.

He also warns individuals seeking investments in second or retirement homes to obtain the advice of a good, capable attorney and to carefully investigate the background, experience, and responsibility of the seller and the particular type of trust agreement of which he will be a beneficiary.

VENTURING WITH MEXICAN CAPITAL

Maurice A. Hall, Beverly Hills real estate entrepreneur, has been investing American capital in Mexican real estate projects since 1972. Investor profit potential is exemplified by a $25 million resort-lot sale project that Hall structured on the Jalisco coast.

While Hall's joint-venture participation was in accordance with investment law, Mexican capital contribution measured by the appraised fair market value of the land to the venture was approximately two-thirds of the total, although the U.S. investor and promoter had a combined 49% interest. Hall developed a funding program with the landowner and a Mexican bank acting as trustee that significantly improved the U.S. investor's position. The pro-forma profit projection is a 16:1 return on investment, with all invested capital returned in the third year of the project. By the seventh year of the program Hall anticipates each limited partner-investor will have received a return of nearly three times his initial investment, with all profits being distributed over a 16-year period. The projection calls for no distribution of profits to the promoter until the seventh year.

Hall projects that the cash needs of the project will be met by receivables financing after sales commence. To conform to Mexican banking requirements, borrowing has been programmed in a series of two-year, 10% notes initially secured by improved land.

The project is unique in relation to most Mexican installment lot sales, because more than 75% of the sales are projected to be made to Mexican citizens. The development is at Bahia Chamela, a four-mile sandy bay on the new coastal highway midway between Puerto Vallarta and Manzanillo, which has a new jet airport approximately 35 miles to the South. The 4000-acre site, which has 4000 feet of white-sand beach, has been master planned primarily for single-family residential use, with an appropriate mix of multiple-residential and commercial zoning.

With a minimum lot size of 6000 square feet, approximately 3400 single-family lots are priced from $5000 to $12,000; the average sales price is $7000. "This price range is well below the range of the seven most nearly comparable offerings on the Baja and mainland coast and is designed to reach the broadest possible economic market consistent with a quality development," Hall says. "This permits penetration of both the Mexican and U.S. markets, particularly the Mexican-American communities in the Southwest. In the pro-forma projections sales prices were based on opening prices, with no allowance for across-the-board increases that typify successful projects or for the added value of multiple-residential and commercial lots."

Installment sales for Phase I of Bahia Chamela are projected to be 10% down, with monthly payments of 1% of the sales price, including 8½% interest on the unpaid balance. "This should be especially appealing in the Mexican market, where interest rates of 12–14% are common," Hall comments.

According to Hall, the project includes paved streets, curbs and gutters, sidewalks, street lighting, and sewer, water, and underground utilities. Because an 18-hole golf course is scheduled for construction approximately six miles from the property, Hall proposes to concentrate on marine amenities, which may include a salt-water marina.

Initial projections were based only on lot sales, but both single-family and condominium residential construction and sales programs, are to be considered later.

Hall screened dozens of properties in Mexico before deciding to proceed with the Bahia Chamela project, largely to determine the true ownership of the land and the ability of a partner to deliver title to the land he contributes to the venture. "It is equally as important to select the right partner for a venture as it is to select the right land," Hall cautions.

BUYING AN ISLAND IN THE SUN

Ford R. Carter, Jr., of Delray Beach, Florida, has been an investor, developer, and sales agent in island property in the Bahamas and the West Indies for more than 25 years. Carter has pioneered development projects and has even sold entire islands.

"Some big profits were made in the late 1950s," Carter affirms, "and there still are excellent opportunities available today."

Carter cites one 400-acre island that was purchased in 1958 for $56,000 and was sold eight months later for $275,000. Another island was purchased for $70,000, sold for $140,000, and resold for $280,000, all within a one-year period.

Carter comments:

It is hard not to become emotionally impressed with the islands in the area, because of the climate, clear water, and beautiful beaches. However, one must remember that island development is a very real specialty.

When you buy land in Florida you have a lot of areas to choose from. Here it is a matter of location, location, location. When you get out in the Atlantic you try to eliminate as much risk as you can. It takes an entirely different approach in research and evaluation, because the problems you have to overcome are so different.

We look for a place with an excellent climate, friendly government, and a good tax status, that has a good harbor, a supply of fresh water, and labor supply. We have to consider installing our own utilities for water, electric power, telephone, and waste disposal. In some cases where the property is so remote, we have put in graded or paved roads, an airstrip, and a marina.

Carter and other investors usually form a Bahamian corporate association to purchase the land. "Generally the land can be financed, but loans are not available for the development work necessary before any sales program can begin. If the U.S. government recognizes the country where the development is taking place as a "less developed nation," then generally the corporation can be dissolved after ten years, and the assets of the corporation returned to the individual stockholders are taxed as long-term capital gains."

Carter suggests that any investor or individual considering residency should discuss tax advantages and consequences with a tax attorney or an accountant. "Some islands have no property tax or income tax, and if the person is a U.S. citizen and can qualify as a nonresident, earnings of as much as $25,000 a year may be tax exempt," Carter explains.

When a development program involves a retail-lot sale, Carter plans for a three-year sellout once the marketing program is begun. "Ideally, we figure on selling 33% the first year, about 50% in the second year, and the balance of 17% in the third year," Carter states.

In addition to registering the development program for sale in the United States, Carter has had excellent success in marketing island properties to Europeans, using agents in England, Germany, and Sweden.

THE TURTLE COVE PROJECT

In 1967 Carter formed an association with a group of friends who had acquired approximately 4000 acres of land from the British Government on Providenciales Island in the Turks and Caicos Islands in the British West Indies.

The project, called Turtle Cove, was master planned for 1110 single and multifamily homesites, including apartment, hotel, motel, and commercial sites, mostly an acre or more in size.

Providenciales is a 40-square-mile island, bordered on the North and West Coasts by an 80-mile barrier reef. The Turks and Caicos Islands contain 166 square miles of land on 30 small islands spread over an area of 5000 square miles. The islands are a self-governing British Crown Colony with a governor appointed by the Crown. The local law is patterned after the Common Law of Great Britain. Carter explains:

In laying out the lot sites we followed the contour of the land to take advantage of its natural terrain and waterways and winding creeks that course through the island.

The British government agreed to sell us the land on the basis the Crown would hold title until all improvements were completed and a hotel was built. This was the start of creating a viable economy.

There were 400 natives on the island. The first day we hired 80 to begin construction on the airport, the roads, a deep-water marina, and the hotel. In the early days we formed our own interisland airline and even became the official mail carriers. Now there is commercial air service available four times a week from Florida.

When you pioneer you have to set the stage. You need accommodations and a place for your people to live. Ideally, it is not the hotel you are going to be using for tourist traffic, but that is how we started at Turtle Cove. The hotel has been doing a good business since and affords prospective lot buyers an opportunity to spend several days on the island while making a decision. Approximately 90% of our buyers have seen their lot before making a purchase.

Lots in Turtle Cove were priced as low as $2500 and as high as $22,500 (for ocean-front sites); the price of an average lot was $8500. Buyers receive a 10% discount for cash payment, but they can purchase lots on favorable installment terms of 1% down and 1% a month, including simple interest of 6% on the unpaid balance.

The local government accepted the developers recommendations and adopted the building code used in Florida to ensure quality construction.

Although well water is easily obtainable in some areas of the island, each homeowner must install a fresh-water roof catchment system with cistern storage, which costs approximately $3000. Septic tanks costing about $500 are used for sewage disposal. Individual homeowners are also required to purchase their own generators for electricity, at a cost of $412. A power cooperative was recently formed to deliver electricity almost anywhere on the island.

MARKETING TURTLE COVE

The Turtle Cove project was first registered simultaneously with the State of Florida and with the Office of Interstate Land Sales of the U.S. Department of Housing and Urban Development (HUD), and then with other states. While waiting for federal and state approval to sell lots in the United States, Carter and his associates sold Turtle Cove lots to Europeans.

John P. Holmes, who directs the advertising, publicity, and marketing activities for Ford R. Carter, Inc., states that only selective national advertising is placed and that no direct-mail promotions is used. "We use no WATS-line telephone solicitations, do not accept collect telephone calls, and do not fly anyone free to the island. We encourage prospective buyers to first visit Providenciales before making a decision, and we assist them in helping make reservations. However, they pay all of their own expenses over and back and while they are there. We do not believe in free junkets."

Holmes places one-sixth page advertisements in selected airline and tourist magazines. Respondents are sent descriptive literature on Turtle Cove, lot prices, a site map, required government reports, and other information, provided it can be mailed to the state in question. A quarterly newsletter is published for all buyers, residents, and prospective buyers who ask to be included on the mailing list.

"We consider our promotional effort very low key and want the people to sell themselves on the decision to buy," says Holmes. "Our default ratio is virtually insignificant, and we attribute much of it to our sales program."

ABUNDANT OPPORTUNITIES

Many other opportunities are available for buyers who wish to purchase resort or recreational property outside the United States.

Guatemala is currently attracting investors who are interested in the development or purchase of a retirement or second home.

Seven Keys Limited has a project on North Caicos called Whitby Haven, where retail lots start at $4800 an acre.

The GAC Corporation has a time-shared condominium project at Cape Eleuthera, the outermost island of the Bahamas. Individuals can purchase selected weeks to personally experience the ownership of a condominium in the resort community. GAC also offers land to builders on which they can develop their own homes for sale, taking advantage of the GAC umbrella promotional efforts.

Canadian Estate Land Company of Toronto, Ontario, markets lakefront and other vacation properties in most of the Canadian provinces.

Any individual who is considering the purchase of foreign land for personal use should first obtain and carefully read the HUD Property Report, as well as any public offering statement certain states require. A development partner should have a thorough knowledge of the government, language, and customs of the country. Local professional counsel can give advice on title search and deed transfers; whether there are particular taxes for deed transfer or registration; tax advantages or disadvantages; who is to own the timber rights and the mineral rights; provisions for resale or subdivision of the land; how any entity for acquisition should be structured; whether there will be any problems inherent in construction, regarding zoning, building codes, or environmental restrictions; and whether architectural covenants are a protection or a deterrent to a buyer.

APPENDIX

LAND MEASUREMENTS

The following information on land measurements is published with the permission of Title Insurance and Trust, Pioneer National Title Insurance, and Ticor Title Insurers, all member companies of The TI Corp.

THE U.S. RECTANGULAR SYSTEM OF SURVEYING

Under an ordinance of the Continental Congress, passed May 20, 1785, the first public land surveys in the United States were made in Ohio in 1786. The system of surveying used is described briefly in this Appendix.

Starting Point. An *initial monument* is established by astronomical observation. This is usually a prominent point or a natural monument that is visible from distant points. From the initial monument, a true North and South line and a true East and West line are established on true parallels of latitude and longitude, respectively. Both the East and West line (the *base*) and the North and South line (the *principal* or *prime meridian*) intersect at the initial monument. The prime meridian is a straight line, whereas the base line follows the earth's curvature.

Parallels. Because of the curvature of the earth, additional lines, called *guide meridians,* run every 24 miles East and West of the prime meridian. Other lines, called *standard parallels,* run every 24 miles North and South of the base line. These guide meridians and standard parallels are also known as *correction*

Diagram of a tract, showing the established base line and prime meridian and the division into ranges and townships.

lines. Parallels North of the base line are designated first standard parallel North, second standard parallel North, and so on. Parallels South of the base line are called first standard parallel South, second standard parallel South, and so on. It was once permissible to place parallels at intervals of 30–36 miles, but if present conditions require additional standard lines, then a new correction line could be established.

Ranges and Townships.   Lines 6 miles apart are then run North on the prime meridian from the standard parallel. This divides the surveyed area into 6-mile-wide strips called *ranges,* which are numbered East and West from the

Sectional map showing six typical townships. Each of the six townships is marked clockwise by the numbers 1, 36, 31, and 6 (one number for each of the four corners).

prime meridian. Similar lines run at 6-mile points North and South of the base line and parallel to the base line cut the ranges into 6-mile squares called *townships* (see Chart A).

The first township North of the base line is numbered township 1 North; the second, township 2 North; and so on. Townships South of the base line are numbered township 1 South, township 2 South, and so on.

Sections.   Townships are divided into 36 parts called *sections.* Each section is one-mile square, *or the nearest equivalent.* The 36 sections in each township are numbered 1–36, beginning with the northeast corner and proceeding West and East, alternately, through the township (see Chart B). In some states sections 16 and 36 in every township are set aside for the construction of schools.

The sections are the smallest tracts required in the survey act, but the sections are further subdivided into four *quarters* that contain approximately 160 acres apiece. These subdivisions are designated the northeast quarter, the northwest quarter, the southeast quarter, and the southwest quarter. The earth's curvature and unavoidable miscalculations cause the sections along the

The progressive subdivision of a section.

North and West boundaries of each township to be irregular. The quarters along the North and West boundaries of these sections take up the excess shortage in the township. The quarter quarters along the North and West township boundaries are given *lot numbers*. Examples are: Lot 2, Section 5, township 11 South, range 3 West, and Lot 7, Section 31, township 11 South, range 3 West.

In some states a township is often partially occupied by Spanish- or Indian-grant land. U.S. government surveys do not cover such grants and are made only to and including their boundaries.

Fractional quarter quarters in the sections created by reason of a grant line are given government numbers at the time of the survey (for example, Lot 2, Section 26, township 11 South, range 4 West). Chart C shows the progressive subdivision of a section.

In addition, when the meander line of a body of water is a boundary or when a section or a township contains an excess or a deficiency caused by natural error, the fractional quarter quarters created are called *section lots*. In short, a lot exists solely for the purpose of describing sectional property that cannot be designated a true quarter section, or 40 acres.

An *acre* is:

$$43,560 \text{ ft}^2$$
$$165 \text{ ft} \times 264 \text{ ft}$$
$$198 \text{ ft} \times 220 \text{ ft}$$
$$5280 \text{ ft} \times 8.25 \text{ ft}$$
$$2640 \text{ ft} \times 16.50 \text{ ft}$$
$$1320 \text{ ft} \times 33 \text{ ft}$$
$$660 \text{ ft} \times 66 \text{ ft}$$
$$330 \text{ ft} \times 132 \text{ ft}$$
$$160 \text{ square rods}$$
$$208 \text{ ft}^2 \, 8\tfrac{1}{2} \text{ in.}^2, \text{ or } 208.71033 \text{ ft}^2$$

Or the product of the length and width that totals 43,560 ft^2 for any rectangular tract.

Table of Land Measurements

Linear Measure			Square Measure		
7.92 in.	=	1 link	$30\tfrac{1}{4}$ yd^2	=	1 square rod
25 links	=	$16\tfrac{1}{2}$ ft	16 square rods	=	1 square chain
25 links	=	1 rod	1 square rod	=	$272\tfrac{1}{4}$ ft^2
100 links	=	1 chain	1 square chain	=	4356 ft^2
$16\tfrac{1}{2}$ ft	=	1 rod	4840 yd^2	=	1 acre
$5\tfrac{1}{2}$ yd	=	1 rod	640 acres	=	1 square mile
4 rods	=	100 links	1 section	=	1 square mile
66 ft	=	1 chain	1 township	=	36 square miles
80 chains	=	1 mile	1 township	=	6 miles square
320 rods	=	1 mile			
5280 ft	=	1 mile			
1760 yd	=	1 mile			

GLOSSARY

Abstract of Title. A condensed history, summary, or digest of the conveyances, transfers, and all transactions affecting a particular tract of land, including any other elements of record that may impair the title.

Accelerated Depreciation. A method of accounting in which income is written off at a greater rate than the ordinary depreciation of a property. Accelerated depreciation is most commonly applied to improvements such as multifamily rental, commercial, or industrial projects.

Acceleration Clause. A provision in a note, deed of trust, or mortgage specifying the conditions under which the lender may advance the time when the entire debt is to become due. For example, the lender has the right to demand that all sums owed him be immediately due and payable on the sale of the property or the failure of a borrower to meet interest payments or installments of principal and interest.

Access. The right to enter and to leave a tract of land from a public way. Often the right to enter and to leave over another's land.

Accommodation Party. A person who signs a note on behalf of another person without receiving any consideration.

Accretion. The slow and gradual building up of land by natural forces, such as wind, wave, or water.

Acknowledgment. The act by which a party executing a legal document declares the same to be his voluntary act and deed before an authorized officer or a notary public.

Acre. A tract of land 208.71 ft² that contains 4840 yd², or 43,560 ft², or 160 square rods of land.

Administrator. A person appointed by a probate court to settle the affairs of an individual dying without a will. If the person is a woman, she is called an *administratrix.*

Ad Valorem. Literally "according to the value," (ad valorem taxes on real property, for example).

Advance Billings. Also called *progress billings* or *retentions.* An amount is withheld from advance billings by the party receiving services to ensure the final and satisfactory completion of the job.

Adverse Possession. A claim made against the land of another by virtue of open and notorious possession of said land by the claimant.

Affiant. One who swears to or affirms the statement in an affidavit.

Affidavit. A sworn statement in writing.

Affirmative Coverage. The provisions in a title insurance policy in which the insurer affirmatively insures a party against loss due to specific risks generally not covered by such policies (loss due to violations of restrictive covenants, for example).

After-completion Costs. Costs incurred for the development of real property after the regular construction period is complete.

Agreement of Sale. A written contract or agreement between a seller and a purchaser stating the terms and conditions of the sale.

Air Rights. The right to ownership or to the use of everything above the physical surface of the land.

AITD. The *All-Inclusive Trust Deed*, subordinate to but including the encumbrances to which it is subordinated (the underlying loans). A device similar to a sales contract that is used to preserve the favorable terms of underlying loans and to provide other financial and tax advantages to the parties concerned. The difference between the all-inclusive loan and the underlying loan is sometimes referred to as an *effective second lien.* Kenneth Leventhal & Company cites the example of a person who sells real property that is encumbered by a first lien of $400,000 for a price of $500,000. The seller retains his liability on the first lien (the underlying loan) and accepts an AITD from the buyer for $450,000 and $50,000 cash. The buyer makes payments to the seller on the AITD; the seller in turn continues to make payments on the $400,000 underlying loan. The

$50,000 difference between the first lien and the underlying loan is the amount of the effective second lien, which also may be called a wraparound; an all-inclusive loan; a hold-harmless trust deed; an overriding trust deed; or an all-inclusive mortgage.

Alienation.   The transfer of property and possession of land or other things from one person to another.

Alienation Clause.   An acceleration clause.

All-inclusive Mortgage.   Essentially the same as an AITD or an all-inclusive trust deed, except that the mortgage instrument is used.

All-inclusive Rate.   A term used in title insurance and the system of quoting insurance rates to indicate that the stated rate includes the cost of title search, the title examination, and the policy. This is in contrast to the system that quotes the rate charged for the policy only. In the latter system the cost of search and examination is additional.

ALTA.   The *A*merican *L*and *T*itle *A*ssociation, a national organization of title insurance companies, abstractors, and attorneys who specialize in real property law.

Amenities.   Attractive improvement features of a piece of property (a tennis court, swimming pool, golf course, etc.).

Amortization.   The periodic reduction of the principal sum of a note or mortgage, payable over the life term of the note or mortgage.

Ancillary Income.   Any income from a project that is in addition to rent.

Annual Constant Payment.   A combination of interest and loan amortization payments expressed as a percentage of the principal sum of the debt.

Anticipation.   The economic principle that value is created by benefits that are to be derived in the future. In real estate this is the theory that the worst house in a given neighborhood will benefit from the greater values of surrounding houses. The opposite of regression.

Appraisal.   An estimate of the real or market value of a specific piece of property in terms of dollar value as of a specific date. An appraisal is based on such factors as comparable sales or reproduction costs and the price a willing buyer would pay a willing seller, supported by factual and relevant data.

Appraiser.   One qualified by experience, education, and training to conduct appraisals.

Appreciation.   An increase in value caused by economic factors or inflation.

Approved Attorney.   An attorney approved by a title insurance company, whose opinions of title are deemed acceptable by the company and who is relied on to issue title insurance policies.

Appurtenance.   Anything so annexed to another thing or to land, or used with it, that is conveyed with the land.

Assessed Valuation.   The valuation placed on property as a basis for taxation; usually a percentage of the market value of the property.

Assessment.   The imposition of a tax, charge, or levy, usually according to established rates.

Assessor.   A public official who evaluates property for the purpose of taxation.

Assignee.   One to whom a transfer of interest is made, such as the assignee of a mortgage or a contract.

Assignment.   A transfer of any property, real or personal, from one person to another.

Assignor.   One who makes an assignment, such as the assignor of a mortgage or a contract.

Assumption Agreement.   Undertaking or adopting a debt or an obligation that rests primarily on another person. The assumer becomes primarily liable, and the original debtor becomes secondarily liable.

Assumption Fee.   The fee paid to a lender that results from the assumption of a mortgage; usually paid by the grantee.

Assumption of Mortgage.   An obligation undertaken in which the purchaser of property assumes liability for payment of an existing note secured by a mortgage or a deed of trust against the property or becomes a coguarantor for the payment of a mortgage or a deed of trust.

Attachment.   Legal seizure of property to force payment of a debt.

Attorney in Fact. One who holds a power of attorney from another giving him the right to execute legal documents (deeds, mortgages, etc.) on behalf of the grantor.

Balloon Mortgage, Balloon Payment. A term generally used to indicate that the final payment on a note or a mortgage is made in a lump sum or that the final payment is greater than any preceding payment; paying the debt obligation in full at the end of a specified term.

Bankrupt. A person, corporation, or entity who is relieved in a court proceeding of the payment of all debts after surrendering all assets to a court-appointed trustee.

Beneficiary. One who is designated to receive the benefit of a trust.

Betterment. A property improvement that increases property value, in contrast to repairs or replacements that do not change the original character or cost of the property.

Binder. An enforceable agreement stating that on satisfaction of the requirements stated in the binder, a title insurer will issue the specified title insurance policy, subject only to the exceptions stated in the binder and setting forth status of title as of a particular date. A deposit paid to secure the right to purchase property at terms previously agreed on by the buyer and the seller.

Blanket Mortgage. A lien on more than one parcel or unit of land, frequently incurred by subdividers or developers who have purchased a single tract of land for the purpose of dividing it into smaller parcels for sale or development.

Blighted Area. Generally, a term applied in redevelopment or urban renewal to indicate an area in which planning, redevelopment, sale of land, and other functions allowed and deemed necessary are designated according to state law.

Blue-sky Laws. State laws designed to protect the public against securities frauds.

Bona Fide. Acting in good faith, without deceit or fraud.

Bond. An insurance agreement in which one party becomes surety to pay (within stated limits) a financial loss caused another party by a specified act or default of a third party. An interest-bearing security evidencing a long-term debt, issued by a government or corporation and sometimes secured by a lien on property.

Breakeven Point. The income required to cover the operating expenses, debt service, vacancy, and other costs when referring to income-producing real property.

Building Line or Setback. A line fixed at a certain distance from the front and/ or sides of a lot, or at certain distances from a road or street, marking the boundary of an area within which no part of any building may project. This line may be established by a filed plat of subdivision, by a restrictive covenant in a deed or lease, by a building code, or by a zoning ordinance.

Bundle of Rights. Beneficial interests or rights, such as access rights, the right to sell, rent, donate, and so on.

Bureau of Land Management. The government office responsible for surveying public lands.

Burnoff. Usually the amortization of front-end prepayments, such as prepaid interest.

Buyer's Closing Costs. The escrow costs to the buyer, including his share of prorated costs, the cost of a title insurance policy, and so on.

Buyer's Commitment. The cash or other valuable consideration given by the buyer in a transaction as a part of either his initial investment (down payment, prepaid interest, etc.) or his continuing commitment. This consideration may be in the form of a letter of credit, payment to a third party to reduce a previously existing debt, or even labor performed by the buyer on the subject property without compensation.

Buy-out Estimate. The projected cost of a structure based on the price of jobs for which contracts have been completely let.

Capitalization. Determination of present value by a series of anticipated future annual installments of income, discounted to a present worth at a specific rate of interest.

Capitalization Rate. The current rate of return derived from dividing the net income of the property by its estimated value.

Carrying Charges. Costs incurred by a developer, primarily interest on land and construction loans and property taxes to carry the property.

Cash Flow. The income that remains after all operating expenses and debt services have been paid.

Cash-on-cash Return. The rate of return on an investment; measured by the cash returned to the investor without considering any tax savings.

Categorical Programs. Grants from the federal government to assist state and local governments in solving specific problems, such as water supply, sewage disposal, urban redevelopment, and renewal programs.

CC&Rs. Covenants, Conditions, and Restrictions that define how a piece of real property can be used and any restrictions on its use.

Certificate of Occupancy. A written authorization from a governing municipality declaring that a newly completed or a substantially completed structure can be inhabited and used.

Certificate of Reasonable Value (CRV). A certificate issued by the Veterans Administration specifying the maximum loan on a given property that is to be guaranteed to an eligible purchaser.

Certificate of Title. A written opinion by an attorney that ownership of a particular parcel of land is as stated in his certificate.

Chain. A unit of land measurement; 66 ft in length.

Chain of Title. A history of past transactions and documents affecting the title to a particular piece of property.

Chattel Mortgage. A personal property mortgage.

Chattel Real. An estate related to real estate, such as a lease on real property.

CD. A Certificate of Deposit issued by a lending institution that enables money deposited for a specified period of time to earn special interest rates not available in passbook savings accounts.

Clear Title. A title that is not encumbered or burdened with defects.

Closing. The process by which all parties involved in a real estate transaction conclude the details of a sale or mortgage. Closing includes the signing and transfer of documents and the distribution of funds, as well as the conditional description of real property by courses and distances at the boundary line, where the lines meet to include the entire land tract.

Cloud on Title. A phrase that indicates an encumbrance on real property (usually on relatively unimportant items) that cannot be removed without a quit-claim deed or court action.

Coinsurance. Insurance when more than one insurer shares part of a single risk; insurance of a risk with another party. Coinsurance is normally implemented by separate companies issuing individual insurance contracts; each company undertakes a fractional part of the whole risk.

Collateral. Marketable real or personal property that a borrower pledges as security for a loan. In mortgage transactions, specific land is the collateral.

Commercial Acre. The term applied to the remainder of an acre of newly subdivided land after the area devoted to streets, sidewalks, curbs, and so on, has been deducted.

Commitment Fee. The fee a potential borrower pays to a potential lender (usually a percentage of the expected loan) for the lender's promise to lend in the future.

Commitment to Insure. A report issued by a title insurance company or its agent that indicates the condition of the title and commits the title insurance company to issue the form policy designated in the commitment, on compliance with and satisfaction of requirements set forth in the commitment.

Common Areas. Land or improvements existing for the benefit of all property owners or tenants, such as those defined in a condominium or a planned-unit or some other development, including parks and playgrounds, swimming pools, garage and parking areas, and so on.

Community Apartment Project. A subdivision that is usually operated, maintained, and controlled by a governing board elected by the owners of the fractional interests. An undivided interest in the property is conveyed, coupled with the right to occupy a certain unit or apartment.

Community Property. A form of property ownership that exists in some states that differs from joint tenancy or tenancy in common. All property acquired in marriage is owned in common by husband and wife, except when acquired as the separate property of either spouse.

Comparables. An appraisal term used to compare properties with similar economic characteristics to indicate the approximate fair market value of the subject property.

Completed Contract Method. A method of recording income from a construction contract on completion of the project.

Condemnation. The act of taking private property for public use in a court proceeding.

Condition. A qualification annexed to an estate that enlarges or deflates the estate when it is met. A condition in a deed may empower the grantor to terminate the interest conveyed if a violation of the condition occurs.

Conditional Commitment. The commitment of a loan of definite amount to some future unknown purchaser with a satisfactory credit standing.

Condominium. A system of individual-fee ownership of units in a multifamily or a multiunit structure, in combination with the joint ownership of common areas of the structure and the land. Each unit is separately mortgaged, and each owner contributes a share of the maintenance and operating expenses of the common areas and facilities.

Conservator. A person appointed by the court to protect and preserve the lands and property of an individual who is physically incapacitated or otherwise unable to handle his own personal affairs.

Construction Costs. Direct costs to improve raw land, in contrast to land, finance, and sales costs.

Construction Loan. Financing (usually short-term loans) arranged for the development of real property.

Construction Loan Draw. Partial funding of a construction loan.

Constructive Notice. A notice given by public record.

Continuing Commitment. The consideration given by a buyer in a transaction after his initial investment. This normally takes the form of regular payments that fully amortize the debt instrument held by the seller over a reasonable period.

Contract. An agreement to sell and purchase in which title is withheld from the purchaser until the required payments to the seller are complete.

Contract Rent. The rent stated in the lease or the rental agreement.

Contract Zoning. The imposition of conditions on a land parcel by a governing body prior to granting a zoning change for the parcel.

Conventional Loans. Loans made by private institutions that are not guaranteed or insured by a government agency.

Convey. The act of deeding or transferring title from one person to another.

Conveyance.   An instrument by which title to property is transferred; a deed.

Cooperative.   Stock ownership in a multiunit building, owned by and operated for the benefit of the tenants, that entitles the stockholder to occupy but not own a unit.

Cost-plus Contract.   A construction contract in which the contract price is equal to the cost of construction plus a profit allowance for the builder.

Cotenancy.   Ownership of the same interest in a particular parcel of land by more than one person, such as tenancy in common, joint tenancy, tenancy by the entireties.

Covenant.   An agreement contained in a deed or other instrument that promises the performance or nonperformance of certain acts or that stipulates certain uses or nonuses of the property.

Credit Report.   A report to a prospective lender concerning the credit standing of the prospective borrower; often requested by the lender-seller regarding the borrower-buyer in conjunction with the escrow.

Cul de Sac.   The terminus of a street or an alley, usually designed by modern engineers to provide a circular turnaround for vehicles.

Curtail Schedule.   A listing of the amounts by which the principal sum of an obligation is to be reduced by partial payments and of the dates when each payment is to become payable.

Curtesy.   The interest in the lands of a wife that is granted a husband by force of law.

Debenture.   A promissory note backed by the general credit of a company and usually not secured by a mortgage or lien on any specific asset.

Debt Service.   The cost of completely repaying a loan; the amount necessary to amortize a loan (the sum of the principal and interest).

Dedication.   The appropriation of land by its owner for some public use that is accepted by authorized public officials.

Deed.   A written legal document transferring the ownership of land from one person to another.

Deed in Lieu.   A deed given by an owner-debtor in lieu of foreclosure by the lender-mortgagee.

Deed of Trust. Conveyance of a land title by the maker of a note (the debtor) to a third party (a trustee) as collateral security for payment of the note, subject to the condition that the trustee is to reconvey title to the debtor on payment of the note. The trustee is empowered to sell the land or property to pay the note if the debtor defaults.

Default. The failure to perform or fulfill a duty or a promise or to discharge an obligation; the omission or failure to perform any act.

Defeasance Clause. A mortgage clause giving the mortgagor the right to redeem his property on payment of his obligations to the mortgagee.

Deferred Payment Sale. A sale in which the proceeds are to be received in more than one payment.

Deficiency Judgment. Any judgment against a person liable for the debt secured by a mortgage in an amount that is more than the funds derived from a foreclosure or a trustee's sale.

Delivery. The final and absolute transfer of a deed from the seller to the buyer in a manner that cannot be recalled by the seller.

Depreciation. A decrease in the value of real property that is caused by age, physical deterioration, or functional or economic obsolescence. In accounting, depreciation is the systematic but arbitrary method of providing for the amortization or write-off of the cost of the asset over its estimated useful life.

Deterioration. The impairment of condition. One of the causes of depreciation, reflecting the decreasé in value of real property as a result of daily wear and tear, disintegration, use in service, and the natural elements.

Devise. The disposition of land by a will; never applied to personal property.

Directional Growth. The location or direction toward which the residential sections of a city are destined or determined to grow.

Discount Points. The amount of money the borrower or the seller must pay the lender to obtain a mortgage at a stated interest rate. This amount is equal to the difference between the principal balance on the note and the lesser amount that the purchaser would pay the original lender for the note under market conditions. One discount point equals 1% of the loan (for example, one point on a $30,000 loan would be $300; two points would be $600; etc.).

Disintermediation. The outflow of funds from thrift institutions to other types of investments; generally caused by fluctuations in the interest rate paid on deposits.

Dower. An estate for life to which a married woman is entitled by statute on the death of her husband. In most states a dower is a life estate of one-third the value of all land that the husband owned during the marriage. Dower has been abolished by statute in some states. A wife is required by law to join in the deed of any land by her husband to release her dower right.

Earnest Money. A deposit that is an advance payment of part of the purchase price a potential buyer pays to a seller to bind a property contract. The deposit can be in the form of money or collateral.

Easement. A right, privilege, or interest that entitles the holder to a specific, limited use, of the land owned by another for the purpose of utilities, ingress or egress, or some other stated use.

Economic Indication of Value. An appraisal technique in which the value of capital goods or real property is determined by an attempt to establish the present worth of the future potential benefits of a property on a given current date.

Economic Rent. The optimum rent a unit would bring if it were rented on the current open market, or the fair rental value of a unit.

Egress. The right to leave a tract of land; also the access to leave.

Eminent Domain. The power of a government to possess private property for necessary public or quasi-public use on payment of a fair and just compensation.

"Empty Nester" Development. A residential project created for the lifestyles of families who have no children or families whose children are already grown and no longer live at home.

Enabling Legislation. A grant of power, usually by a state legislature, to a political subdivision that authorizes the enactment of certain laws and regulations.

Encroachment. A fixture, such as a house, wall, or fence, that illegally intrudes on the property of another.

Encumbrance. A lien, liability, or charge that affects or limits the fee-simple title to property.

Endorsement. A form issued by the insurer at the request of the insured that changes the term(s) or item(s) in an issued policy or a commitment for title insurance.

Environmental Impact Report. A report commonly required by many local governments and agencies that evaluates the impact and the effect of a particular type of development on the local environment by anticipating changes in nature, ecology, resources, and pollution and by discussing both the advantages and the disadvantages of development.

Equity. The interest or the value that an owner has invested in real estate in addition to the debts against the property.

Equity Participation. A type of transaction in which the lender not only receives a fixed rate of interest on the loan but also has an interest in and a share in the profits of the borrower's project. Also called a *kicker*; accepted by brokers, syndicators, and other real estate professionals as consideration for services rendered.

Equity of Redemption. The right to redeem property during the foreclosure period; for example, a mortgagor's right to redeem property within a year after the foreclosure sale.

Escalator Clause. A contract provision for the upward or downward adjustment of certain items to cover specified contingencies, such as attaching operating costs or property taxes to a lease or specifying rates based on a cost of living index.

Escheat. The reversion of property to the state in cases when an individual dies without heirs or devisees and without a will.

Escrow. A procedure in which instruments, legal documents, and funds are deposited with a disinterested third party, who is given instructions to carry out the provisions of an agreement or a contract on behalf of the seller and the buyer.

Escrow Costs. All the costs to the buyer and the seller, individually, that are associated with a transaction.

Escrow Holder. The person or organization with the fiduciary responsibility to both the buyer and the seller (or the lender and the borrower) to ensure that the terms of the transaction are fulfilled.

Escrow Instructions. Instructions given to the escrow holder by the parties involved concerning the terms and conditions of a transaction. Escrow instructions can but do not necessarily supercede the terms of the deposit receipt; in some cases these instructions constitute a valid contract of sale.

Escrow Statement. A document that is given (for example) to the buyer and the seller at the escrow closing, itemizing the terms and associated costs of the sale.

Estate. The degree, quantity, nature, and extent of interest that a person has in real property; also a person's possessions.

Estate for Years. An interest in lands by virtue of a contract for their possession for a definite and limited period of time. A lease in an estate for years.

Exception. In legal descriptions, that portion of lands to be deleted or excluded; an objection to title or an encumbrance on title.

Exclusionary Zoning. The use of zoning tools by a community or a local government to prevent the development of specific types of residential property or to prevent a particular segment of the population from residing in the community; discriminatory zoning.

Exclusive Agency Listing. A written instrument that gives one agent the right to sell a given property for a specified time but reserves the owner's right to sell the property himself without paying the agent a commission.

Exclusive Right to Sell Listing. A written agreement between an owner an an agent that grants the agent the right to collect a commission if the property is sold by anyone during the term of the agreement.

Exculpatory Clause. The provision in a financial instrument, agreement, or contract stating that the debtor is not to be held personally liable if he defaults.

Fair Market Value. The price a given property would bring if it were sold on the current open market, presuming that a reasonable amount of time were taken to find a buyer aware of all the potential uses and capabilities of the property.

Fee or Fee Simple. The absolute ownership of real property, which is not limited in duration, disposition, or descendability; the opposite of a leasehold interest.

Finance Costs. The costs (usually limited to interest and loan fees) that are incurred in financing the construction of a project.

Financing Statement. A document filed with the Register of Deeds or the Secretary of State indicating that personal property or fixtures is/are encumbered with a debt.

First Mortgage Loan. A first lien against property, usually contracted to provide real estate financing for a long period of time.

Fixed Disbursement Schedule. The disbursement system in a construction loan in which the lender and the borrower agree on the number of payments to be made during the construction period and at which stages these payments are to be made.

Fixed Price Contract. A construction agreement in which a specific contract price is agreed on before construction begins.

Fixtures. Any personal property that is attached to land or improvements and considered part of the real property.

Foreclosure. The legal process by which a mortgagor of real property is deprived of his interest in that property because he has failed to comply with the terms and conditions of the mortgage. The legal proceeding when a lender redeems property from a mortgage or who has failed to make regular payments.

Forfeiture. The loss of money or anything of value as a result of the failure to comply with previously accepted conditions.

Formal Closing. The legal transfer of title from a seller to a buyer.

Frontage. The front boundary line of a lot facing the street.

Front Foot. A measure of lot size related to the width of the lot at the street; generally used to determine the value of commercial property.

Front Money. Capital required, costs incurred, or money paid at the beginning of a project, transaction, or agreement for land, permanent financing fees, and legal or other fees not normally included in a construction loan. Also called *seed money* or *start-up costs.*

Gap Financing. A loan granted to fulfill a borrower's temporary needs until a permanent loan can be extended. For example, a lender may require a minimum occupancy level in a new apartment building before he grants the developer a permanent loan; to fill the "gap" between his interim and permanent financing, the developer must secure gap financing.

General Contractor. The person who performs and supervises the construction of an improvement or a development.

General Warranty Deed. A deed that contains a covenant in which the seller promises to protect the buyer against dispossession from any adverse claim.

Gift Deed. A deed granted out of consideration, love, or affection, and not for material gain.

Graduated Lease. A lease that provides a varying rental rate, often based on future determinations and periodic appraisals; generally used in long-term leases.

Grant. A technical term used in deeds of land conveyance to indicate a transfer.

Grant Deed. A deed in which the grantor verifies that he has not previously conveyed or encumbered the property. A grant deed is *not* a warranty that the grantor is the owner of the property or that the property is unencumbered. A grant deed also conveys any title acquired later by the grantor, unless a different intent is expressed.

Grantee. A person who acquires an interest in a given property by a deed, a grant, or some other written instrument.

Grantor. A person who, by written instrument, transfers his interest in a given property to another person.

Gross Rent Multiple. A figure used to compare rental properties that indicates the relationship between the rental value and the sales price.

Ground Lease. An agreement for the use of the land only; sometimes secured by improvements placed on the land by the user.

Guardian. A person appointed by the court to administer the affairs of an individual who is not capable of managing them himself.

Hard Money. Money given in exchange for an improved equity or ownership position in a transaction, such as cash down or a down payment, and the principal portion of debt service. Also called *hard dollars*.

Hard-money Equivalents. The sum of hard money and a portion of soft money equal to the amount the payor would not be refunded in tax savings (for example, if the payor is in a 30% tax bracket, his equivalent hard-money payment is equal to the hard money plus 70% of the soft money).

Heir. A person who might inherit or succeed to a land or property interest under the rules of law applicable when an individual dies without leaving a will.

Heirs and Assigns. Terminology used in deeds and wills to enable a recipient to receive a "fee-simple estate" in lands rather than a lesser interest.

Hiatus. A gap or space that may be unintentionally left between adjacent parcels of land when they are described.

Highest and Best use. Use that is most likely to produce the greatest net return at a specific time on the land or structure over a given period of time.

Holdback. The portion of a loan commitment that is not funded until some additional requirement is met.

Homestead. The estate in land that a homeowner holds and that he and his family occupy as their residence. The estate is exempt from forced sale to satisfy the householder's debts.

Hypothecate. To offer something of value as security without having to give it up as a possession.

Impounds. Payments made to a lender or to some other fiduciary that are in addition to the principal and interest portions of the loan amortization (for example, for the purpose of paying property taxes, assessments, and insurance). Impounds offer a lender the additional security that no liens can be imposed on the property on which he has extended a loan.

Improved Land. Land on which onsite or offsite work has been performed; the opposite of raw land.

Improvements. Additions to raw land that tend to increase its value, such as buildings, streets, and utilities.

Imputation of Interest. The use of present value measurements to reevaluate a note when the face amount and the stated interest rate do not reasonably represent the present value of the consideration given or received in the exchange. This circumstance may arise if the note is noninterest bearing or if its stated interest rate differs from the appropriate interest rate for the debt at the date of the transaction.

Inchoate Curtesy. The imperfected interest the law grants a husband in his wife's lands.

Inchoate Dower. The imperfected interest the law grants a wife in her husband's lands. On the death of the husband, this interest can be extended to possession and use.

Infrastructure. Water, sewage, and waste-disposal facilities, utilities, roads, schools, and government or civic facilities in a community.

Ingress. The right to enter a tract of land; also the access to enter.

Injunction. A writ or a legal order issued by a court that restrains one or more parties in a suit or a proceeding from commiting an act deemed inequitable or unjust in regard to the rights of some other party or parties in the suit or proceeding.

In rem Note. A nonrecourse note, such as a purchase-money mortgage or a trust deed.

Installment Note. A note providing that payments of a certain sum or amount are to be paid on dates specified in the instrument.

Insurance of Title. Insurance of ownership of a specified interest in designated real estate that indicates exceptions to the insured interest in the form of defects, liens, and encumbrances existing against that insured interest.

Interest Rate. The percentage rate charged for borrowed money; usually expressed as part of the terms and conditions of a mortgage loan or transaction.

Interim Financing. A construction loan that covers the cost of construction and other incidental expenses that can be attributed to construction.

Intermediate-term Loans. Interim financing on income-producing projects for an average of one to five years and for a maximum of ten years, prior to an arrangement of permanent financing.

Intestate. A term designating the estate or condition of failing to leave a will at death.

Involuntary Lien. A lien imposed against a given property without the owner's consent, such as taxes, special assessments, or judgments.

Joint Protection Policy. A title insurance policy in a form suitable to insure both the owner and the lender.

Joint Tenancy. Joint property ownership, in which two or more persons hold real estate jointly for life, owning equal interest and rights in the property; the survivor acquires (or the survivors divide) the interest of an owner who dies.

Judgment. A court decree, such as the lien or charge on a debtor's property that results from the court's award of money to a creditor.

Judgment Lien. A charge on the property of a debtor resulting from a court decree properly recorded in the recorder's office of the county in which the property is located.

Junior Lien. A lien that is subordinate to another lien.

Junior Mortgage. A mortgage, the lien of which is subordinate to that of another mortgage, such as a *second mortgage*.

Labor and Material Release. A document signed by laborers and materialmen and presented to the developer, which waives their rights under any mechanic's liens.

Land Contract. A contract used in some areas of the country to sell real property on an installment plan, with a small down payment and periodic payments on the principal balance and interest. The title remains with the seller until the terms of the contract are fulfilled.

Land Cost. All costs associated with the purchase of land, including purchase price and recording fees, escrow costs, interest on land loans, and property taxes prior to construction.

Land-development Loan. A loan granted to cover the costs of developing the land; usually secured by a mortgage.

Land Loan. A loan granted to finance the purchase of raw land. A land loan is normally subordinated to or and paid off by the construction loan.

Lease. A contract in which the owner (lessor) and the tenant establish conditions and terms for the rental of real estate.

Leasehold Financing. A loan extended to a lessee on the security of his leasehold estate. Under the terms of some leases, the property owner is required to subordinate to the leasehold; that is, to hypothecate his ownership interest in the property as further security for the loan to the lessee.

Legal Description. A description recognized by law of a given property that enables it to be located on government surveys or approved recorded maps.

Lessee. A person who leases property.

Lessor. A person who grants a lease.

Leverage. The ability to utilize borrowed money to purchase real property.

Lien. The hold, claim, or charge of a creditor on the property of a debtor.

Life Estate. The grant or reservation of an individual's right to use, occupy, and own property for life.

Limited Partnership. A partnership in which some partners' contributions and liabilities are limited.

Link. A unit of land measurement; $\frac{1}{100}$ chain, or $\frac{66}{100}$ ft.

Link Financing. The additional financing a borrower receives to cover the amount of a compensating balance. For example, a lender of $50,000 requires that a compensating balance of $10,000 be held in the borrower's checking account; link financing of $10,000 is the additional requirement that the borrower must fulfill to obtain the $50,000.

Lis Pendens. A notice in the official records of a county indicating that a suit is pending that will affect the lands where the notice is recorded.

Listing. An employment contract between a principal and an agent that authorizes the agent to perform services for the principal involving the latter's property. Listing contracts are entered to secure persons to buy, lease, or rent property. Employing an agent to buy, lease, or locate property for such use may be considered a listing.

Loan Commitment. A lender's written promise to lend an agreed-on sum at a certain rate of interest. Loan commitments are usually paid in fees for a specified length of time.

Loan to Facilitate. A loan extended (often under particularly favorable terms) to facilitate the purchase of real property from the lender; usually a thrift institution with respect to repossessed property.

Loan Fee. The fee paid a lender for his service of extending the loan, or an amount paid in addition to interest (points). Loan fees are generally a percentage of the face amount of the loan.

Loan/Value Ratio. The percentage ratio of the mortgage loan to the appraised value of the property. If a property is valued at $100,000 and a lender approves a $75,000 mortgage, this is a 75% loan/value ratio. If the same lender approves an $80,000 loan, then the loan/value ratio is 80%.

Lock-in Period. A period during which a lender prohibits a borrower from selling or otherwise transferring the property which secures the note or from prepaying any or all of the balance of the note.

Lot. A measured parcel of land with fixed boundaries.

Lot Book. Records maintained by a title company both of the transactions that affect a particular parcel of real property and of every instrument describing the property that are filed with the county in which the property is located.

Majority. The age at which a person is legally entitled to handle his own affairs. Majority varies from state to state.

Marginal Land. Land that barely pays the cost of working or using it.

Margin of Security. The difference between the amount of the mortgage loan(s) and the appraised value of the property.

Marketable Title. A good title about which there is no fair or reasonable doubt.

Market Price. The price paid for property, regardless of pressures, motives, or intelligence.

Master Deed. The basic document used in the creation of a condominium, describing the division of the project into units and common elements.

Materials Bond. Insurance to a contractor that the person posting the bond will provide the materials necessary for the completion of some work.

Mechanics Lien. A lien extended by statute to contractors, laborers, and materials suppliers on improvements and other structures on which they have worked or for which they have supplied materials.

Metes and Bounds. The lengths and directions of the boundaries of a tract of land that is usually irregular in shape.

Mortgage. A legal and conditional instrument used to secure the payment of a debt or an obligation.

Mortgage-backed Securities. Bondlike investment securities issued against a pool of mortgages or trust deeds.

Mortgage Banker.   A firm or an individual acting as a principal, committing its/his own money to a loan, and usually servicing the loan.

Mortgage Broker.   A person who brings the borrower and the lender together and who receives a commission for this service.

Mortgage Commitment.   A formal, written commitment from a lender agreeing to lend a specified amount of money at a specified rate of interest for a specified length of time. A *loan commitment.*

Mortgage Insurance.   Insurance to protect the lender against any financial loss resulting from the mortgagor's default on payment; also *mortgage guaranty insurance, private mortgage insurance.*

Mortgage Release Price.   A prearranged amount that a lender is repaid to relinquish his lien on an individual parcel, usually when it is sold. For example, when a completed house within a subdivision is sold, the mortgage release price is paid to the lender to release his lien on the property.

Mortgagee.   The mortgage lender.

Mortgagor.   The mortgage borrower.

Multiple Listing.   A listing, usually an exclusive right to sell, by a member of an organization composed of real estate brokers.

Negative Cash Flow.   The stream of cash expenditures in connection with the operation of an income-producing property that is in excess of the cash receipts generated by that property.

Net Lease.   A lease that includes a provision that the lessee pay for some direct expenses associated with the leased property, such as taxes, insurance, and maintenance. The term *net-net lease* implies that additional expenses are paid; the term *net-net-net lease* implies that all expenses associated with the leased property are paid by the lessee.

Net Listing.   A listing that provides that the agent may retain as compensation for his services all sums received over and above a net price to the owner.

Net Realizable Value.   The fair market value reduced by the costs of disposition.

Nonrecourse Note.   A debt instrument that grants the lender no personal recourse against the borrower; the lender must depend solely on the property for repayment (for example an *exculpatory clause*).

Notary Public. An official authorized by law to attest to and to certify certain documents by his hand and official seal.

Note. A written promise to pay a certain amount of money at a certain time or in a specified number of installments. A note usually includes interest payments; the payment of a note is sometimes secured by a mortgage.

Notice of Completion. The notice that is recorded after construction is complete. Mechanics liens must be filed within a specified period thereafter, generally 30–60 days.

Notice of Default. A notice recorded after the occurrence of a default under a deed of trust, such as a *foreclosure*.

Notice of Nonresponsibility. Notice given by an owner to relieve the land from mechanics liens under prescribed conditions. The notice usually must be posted on the property and recorded in the county in which the land is located.

Notice to Quit. An eviction notice.

Offsite Costs. Costs incurred in the improvement of raw land that are not associated with the construction of a building, such as curbs, gutters, sidewalks, and streets.

Onsite Costs. Costs incurred for the actual improvement or structure to be situated on the land.

Open-end Loan. Secured loans that provide sums of money to the same borrower at various times.

Open-end Mortgage. A mortgage or a deed or trust written to secure and permit the advancement of funds in addition to the amount originally loaned.

Open Listing. The authorization by a property owner giving a real estate agent the nonexclusive right to secure a purchaser. The owner may give open listings to a number of agents, but he is only required to compensate the first agent who sells the property.

Option. The right to buy property at an agreed-on price within a specified time, binding on the seller if the purchaser pays for the right or gives some form of consideration.

Option Listing. A listing agreement that gives the broker an option to purchase the property.

Over Improvement.   An improvement that is excessive in cost and/or size and therefore not the highest and best use of the site.

Packaging.   Performing or arranging the performance of certain initial development activities, such as market research, land evaluation, land acquisition, project design and concept, architecture, engineering, zoning, and obtaining financing.

Partition.   The division of land, usually by a legal proceeding, among its former coowners.

Patent.   A document that grants public lands to an individual.

Percentage Base or Percentage Lease.   A lease in which the rental is determined by the amount of business conducted by the lessee.

Percentage of Completion Method.   A method of recording income from construction contracts in which income is based on the ratio of costs incurred to date to total estimated construction costs.

Performance Bond.   Insurance that all the work specified in a contract is to be performed by the person posting the bond.

Permanent Loan or Mortgage.   A loan received to finance the purchase or operation of a completed structure.

Personal Property.   Any property that is not real property.

Planned Unit Development (PUD)   A subdivision in which some lots or areas are owned in common and are reserved for the use of some or all the owners of the separately owned lots. The greater flexibility in locating buildings and in combining various land uses often makes it possible to achieve certain economies in construction.

Plat or Plot.   A map representing a piece of land subdivided into lots with streets shown thereon.

Points.   Discount points or a loan fee. A discount point adds approximately $\frac{1}{8}$th% to the yield on a 30-year mortgage; charging 4 points means that .50% is added to the interest rate returned by the loan. A point is a charge of 1% of the mortgage value for a one-time charge to the borrower (1 point on a $20,000 mortgage is $200; 2 points are $400; etc.).

Power of Attorney.   An instrument authorizing another person to act on one's behalf as an agent or attorney.

Preclosing. A transaction preceding formal closing; often used to distinguish between transactions that affect title to real property and events that merely appear to be a formal closing.

Preliminary Public Report. A report usually issued by a state agency on receipt of the filing fee and a subdivision questionnaire filing that is complete except for some particular requirement. If a preliminary public report is issued, the developer can accept a reservation to purchase or lease a lot or parcel in the subdivision, provided the buyer has read the report and has signed a receipt for it and provided the reservation agreement can be canceled by the buyer at any time and his deposit can be refunded in full.

Prepayment Penalty. A penalty for the payment of a mortgage debt before it actually becomes due. The penalty is usually greatest in the first year of the mortgage and decreases percentage-wise in subsequent years to the point in the term of the mortgage beyond which there is no penalty.

Prescription. The doctrine by which easements are acquired by the long, continuous, and exclusive use and possession of property.

Primary Financing. A loan secured by a first mortgage or a trust deed on real property.

Principal. The amount of money borrowed from a lender.

Prorates. Prorated expenses in an escrow between the buyer and the seller, such as dividing property taxes and interest, based on the date of closing of escrow.

Provision for Warranty. A reserve for the possible contingent costs associated with repairing or replacing defective items in new products; generally included in the year of sale as a part of the sales cost.

Public Records. Records that by law impart constructive notice of matters relating to real property.

Public Report. A subdivision report usually issued by a state agency before the sale of lots in a subdivision. The report is a factual account of the subdivided property that emphasizes what might be considered its shortcomings. A public report is not issued until the agency is satisfied that the subdivider has installed promised improvements and facilities or has made satisfactory financial arrangements to assure their completion and to back any warranties or representations.

Purchase-money Mortgage or Trust Deed. A mortgage that the purchaser gives the seller simultaneously with the purchase of real estate to secure the unpaid balance of the purchase price of the property.

Quiet Title. A legal court action brought to remove a cloud on title or to establish title.

Quit-claim Deed. A deed that transfers whatever interest the grantor may have in a particular real estate property at the time the conveyance is executed.

Raw Land. Land that is not improved by any structure or utility or on which no work has been performed.

Real Estate. The physical land or improvements related thereto.

Real Property. The interests, benefits, and rights inherent in the ownership of real estate. Ownership is endowed by the bundle of rights.

Reconveyance. A deed from the mortgagee or trustee of a deed of trust that releases specific property from the lien of the mortgage or deed of trust.

Recording Fee. The fee charged by the county to record the transfer of title from a seller to a buyer.

Recourse Note. A debt instrument that gives a lender personal recourse against the borrower beyond the repossession of security or collateral.

Redemption. In some states the right of an owner to reclaim title to his property if he pays the debt to the mortgagee within a stipulated time after foreclosure.

Reformation. An action to correct a mistake in a deed or other document.

Refundable Utility Contract. A contract between a developer and a local utility company in which the utility agrees to reimburse the developer for costs incurred in the installation of utility extensions (for water, gas, electricity, etc.) from revenues the utility receives.

Regression. An economic principle that value is diminished by disadvantages anticipated in the future. In real estate, the theory that the value of the best house in a given neighborhood is adversely affected by the condition of inferior houses in the same neighborhood.

Reinsurance. The act of an insurer transferring a portion of a risk to other insurers. The original insurer is the sole insurer for a portion of the risk and shares such risk in excess amount with the reinsurers. The first portion of the loss risk retained by the ceding company as its sole liability is called the *primary liability.*

Reissue Rate. A reduced rate of title insurance premium applicable when the property owner has been previously insured in an owner's policy by the insurer within a certain period of time.

Release Clause. A stipulation or clause in a transaction agreement that on payment of a specific sum of money to the holder of a trust deed or mortgage, the lien of the small instrument on a specific described lot or area is to be removed from the blanket lien on the whole area involved.

Releases. In this unmodified form the term usually applies to a release clause in a loan agreement.

Remainder. An interest or estate in land in a person other than the grantor in which the right of possession and enjoyment of the land is postponed until the termination of some other interest or estate in that land.

Rental Concessions. Agreements between a landlord and a tenant to forgive rent in some way. In projecting the expected gross income from a rental property, rental concessions reduce the amount of contract rent specified.

Rent-up Period. The time following the completion of construction during which a rental property reaches its maximum capacity.

Replacement Cost. The cost of producing an item with the same utility, employing modern materials, labor, and techniques.

Replacement Reserve. A cash reserve for the future replacement of fixed assets.

Reproduction Cost. The cost of reproducing an item with identical materials and characteristics.

Restriction. A provision in a deed or will or in a "Declaration of Condition, Reservations, and Restrictions" that limits the right to use land or to convey its title in some way. Examples are building setback lines and limitations on property for residential use.

Retentions. The amount withheld from progress billings or invoices received during construction by the party receiving services to ensure the final and satisfactory completion of the job.

Reversion. A provision in conveyance on the occurrence of an event or a contingency by which title to land or other property is to return to the grantor or his successor in interest in the land or property.

Right of Survivorship. The right to acquire the interest of a deceased joint owner, which is a distinguishing feature of joint tenancy.

Right of Way. A privilege such as an easement that an owner grants by agreeing to give another party ingress or egress to property or land for passage, access, utilities, or some other purpose.

Riparian. Pertaining to the banks of a watercourse. A landowner adjacent to a watercourse is called a *riparian owner,* and the rights of the riparian owner related to the watercourse are *riparian rights.*

Sale-leaseback. A transaction in which a land or property owner sells the property to another buyer but retains the use of the land or property by immediately releasing it for a specified period and rent.

Sales Commission. The fee paid to an agent or a broker for arranging the sale of property; generally, a percentage of the sale price.

Sales Contract. An agreement between a buyer and a seller as to the terms of the transaction.

Sales Costs. The costs incurred for the sales promotion of the entire project.

Sales Deposit Receipt. A form that is not only the acknowledgment of a deposit but may also constitute a contract for the sale and purchase of property when executed by both the buyer and the seller.

Sales Incentives. Additional concessions to the buyer to persuade him to make a purchase.

Secondary Financing. A loan secured by a second mortgage or a trust deed on real property.

Second Mortgage. A mortgage or a deed of trust on property that is subsequent to an existing mortgage and in which the interest of the holder is secondary to the first mortgage holder.

Section or Section of Land. A parcel of land one square mile or 640 acres in area.

Secured Party. The party with a security interest. The mortgagee, the conditional seller, the pledgee, are all individually referred to as the *secured party.*

Security Agreement. An agreement between the secured party and the debtor creating the security interest.

Security Interest. A term that designates the interest of the creditor in the property of the debtor in all types of credit transactions. Security interest replaces such terms as chattel mortgage, pledge, trust receipt, chattel trust, equipment trust, conditional sales, or inventory lien.

Seed Money. Front-end money or money used to start development (preliminary planning, research and evaluation, etc.).

Seller's Closing Costs. Escrow costs to the seller, including his share of prorates, the cost of selling commissions, and so on.

Selling Expenses. Costs incurred for the sale of a particular piece of property.

Sequence Sheet. A list of properties or lots within a project in the order of their development.

Setback Lines. Lines that delineate the required distances for the location of structures in relation to the perimeter of the property.

Settlement Costs. Costs that are different from closing costs but that still involve charges that a buyer or a seller must pay at closing. Settlement costs include insurance and tax payments, special assessments for improvements to municipal facilities, and sales commissions.

Sheriff's Deed. A deed granted by court order in connection with the sale of property to satisfy a judgment.

Soft Money. Money that does not improve the equity position of the payor, such as prepaid interest and the interest portion of the debt service. The opposite of hard money.

Special Assessment. A legal charge against real estate by a public authority levied to pay the cost of public improvements (street lighting, sidewalks, street improvements, etc.).

Special Warranty Deed. A deed that contains a convenant in which the seller agrees to protect the buyer against dispossession resulting from any adverse claims to the land or property by the seller or anyone issuing a claim through him.

Specific Performance. An action that compels the performance of an agreement.

Standby Commitment. A lender's promise to extend a temporary loan to a potential borrower if the borrower is unable to obtain other financing immediately. The commitment is paid for and is usually based on a percentage of the loan desired.

Start-up Costs. Costs incurred at the beginning of a project; usually of a one-time nature.

Subdivision. A tract of land that is surveyed and divided into lots for the purpose of sale or development.

Subject to Mortgage. A term that is applied when a grantee takes title to real property subject to a mortgage and is not responsible to the holder of the promissory note for the payment of any portion of the amount due. The maximum loss that the grantee can sustain in the event of a foreclosure is his equity in the property. The original maker of the note is not released from his responsibility.

Sublease. A secondary lease executed by a lessee to a third person for a shorter term than the remaining term of the original lease. If the term of the sublease is coincident with the remaining term of the original lease, the sublease is the same as an assignment of the lease.

Subordinate. A person who is subject to or junior to another.

Subordination. A term denoting the willingness of a mortgage or a lien holder to accept payment or secondary payment priority after another creditor.

Subrogation. The substitution of another person in place of the creditor, to whose rights in relation to the debt the substitute succeeds. This doctrine is often used when one person agrees to stand surety for the performance of a contract by another person.

Substitution of Liability. The assumption of liability by a grantee on a mortgage or a trust deed note and the concurrent release of the grantor by the mortgagee or beneficiary.

Subsurface Right. The right to ownership of everything beneath the physical surface of the property.

Surety. A person who guarantees the performance of another person.

Survey. The process of measuring land to determine its size, location, and physical description.

Take-out Loan. A permanent loan or mortgage that a lender agrees to extend to a borrower on completion of specified improvements. The proceeds of the loan are primarily used to pay off the construction loan.

Tax Deed. The deed given to a buyer at a public sale for nonpayment of taxes on the purchased property. A tax deed conveys to the purchaser only such title as the defaulting taxpayer held; it does not convey good title to that extent unless statutory procedures for the sale have been strictly followed.

Tax Sale. The sale of property by the taxing authority to satisfy the payment of delinquent taxes.

Tenancy in Common. Ownership by two or more persons who have an undivided interest in a given property without right of survivorship. The ownership interests need not be equal.

Tenant. Any person in possession of real property with the owner's permission.

Tentative Map. A preliminary map of a proposed subdivision that subdividers may be required to submit to a planning commission for study. The approval or disapproval of a planning commission is noted on the map. A final map of the tract embodying any changes requested by the commission is subsequently filed with the planning commission.

Testate. The estate or condition of leaving a will at death.

Testator. A person who makes or who has made a testament or a will; most commonly a man.

Testatrix. A woman who makes or who has made a testament or a will.

Title. The evidence or right that a person has to the ownership and possession of land.

Title Defect. Any legal right held by others to claim property or to make demands on the property owner.

Title Insurance. Insurance against loss or damage resulting from defects or failure of title to a particular parcel of real property.

Title Search. An examination of public records, laws, and court decisions to disclose the current facts regarding ownership of real estate.

Torrents System. A government title registration system wherein title to land is evidenced by a certificate of title issued by a public official known as the *registrar of title.*

Township. A division of territory 6 miles square that contains 36 sections, or 36 square miles.

Tract. In some states a unit of subdivided land numbered and recorded with the county recorder's office.

Tract Administration Costs. Costs incurred for the administration and supervision of the tract construction.

Tract Map. A map indicating the physical boundaries of lots and tracts under development; usually prepared by the developer.

Trade Fixtures. Articles of personal property that are annexed to real property but that are removable by the owner because they are necessary to the owner's trade.

Trust. A right of property that one person holds for the benefit of another person.

Trust Deed. The instrument a borrower gives to a trustee that vests title in the trustee as security for the fulfillment of an obligation (usually the repayment of a loan to a beneficiary).

Trustee. A person holding property in trust.

Trustor. The grantor of property to a trustee.

Underlying Loan. The loan or loans covered by a sales contract or an all-inclusive trust deed.

Unearned Increment. An increase in real estate value that is not the result of an effort on the part of the owner; often the result of an increase in population.

Unimproved Land. Raw land or land that has not been improved.

Usury. Interest that is in excess of the legal rate charged to a borrower for the use of money.

Vacancy Factor. A percentage rate expressing the loss in gross rental income as a result of vacant rental units.

Vendee.   A purchaser of real property.

Vendor.   A seller of real property.

Voluntary Lien.   Any lien placed on property with the consent of or as a result of the voluntary act of the owner.

Voucher System.   In regard to a construction loan, this term applies to the system of giving subcontractors a voucher in lieu of cash; the voucher can be redeemed with the maker of the construction loan.

Walk-away Risk.   Deterrents to a contractual party to default at key points in the life of the project.

Warehousing.   The activity of a lender who holds mortgage or trust deed notes receivable in inventory or in a "warehouse" for future sale; generally accomplished by a mortgage banking company. The purchase of these loans is usually financed by short-term loans that are repaid from the proceeds of the sale of the notes.

Warranty or Warranty Deed.   An agreement by the grantor to defend the premises against the lawful claims of third persons and an assurance that he is the property owner and will defend the title given.

Will.   A written document property witnessed that directs the distribution of property owned by the deceased.

Wraparound Mortgage or Trust Deed.   A mortgage that secures a debt that includes the balance due on an existing senior mortgage and an additional amount advanced by the wraparound mortgagee. The wraparound mortgagee thereafter makes the amortizing payments on the senior mortgages. For example, a landowner has a mortgage securing a debt with an outstanding balance of $2,500,000. A lender now advances the same mortgagor a new $750,000 mortgage and undertakes to make the remaining payments due on the $2,500,000 debt. The lender takes a $3,250,000 wraparound mortgage on the land or property to secure this new note.

Zero Lot Line.   A term normally used to describe the positioning of a structure on a lot, so that one side of the structure rests directly on the boundary line and is not set back.

Zoning.   The act of a governing authority that specifies the uses for which property may be developed in specific areas.

INDEX